Editor
Eric Migliaccio

Illustrator
Mark Mason

Cover Artist
Brenda DiAntonis

Editor in Chief
Ina Massler Levin, M.A.

Creative Director
Karen J. Goldfluss, M.S. Ed.

Art Production Manager
Kevin Barnes

Art Coordinator
Renée Christine Yates

Imaging
Rosa C. See

Publisher

Mary D. Smith, M.S. Ed.

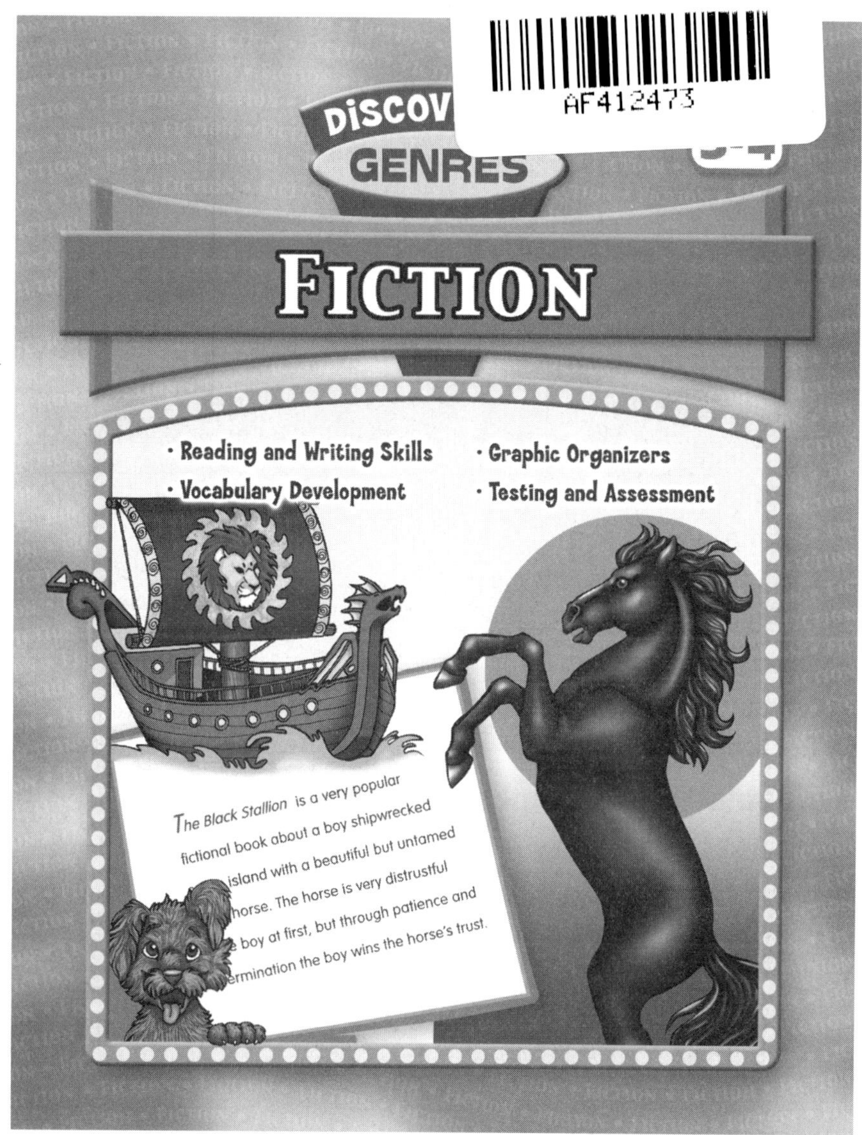

Author

Susan Mackey Collins, M. Ed.

Teacher Created Resources, Inc.
6421 Industry Way
Westminster, CA 92683
www.teachercreated.com

ISBN: 978-1-4206-9052-1

© 2008 Teacher Created Resources, Inc.
Made in U.S.A.

Table of Contents

Table of Contents *(cont.)*

Introduction

Literature is such a wonderful part of language arts. When students are tired of learning about commas and capitalization or spelling and vocabulary, there is always a great story sitting somewhere on a shelf, just waiting to grab the reader, take him on an adventure, and teach him something wonderful. This book, *Discovering Genres: Fiction,* is the perfect companion piece to that adventure.

There are so many different genres available to anyone who wants to read. Sometimes understanding these different literature types takes a bit of extra effort. Many people find a certain genre can be more enjoyable if the reader has some background knowledge about the type of literature he is reading.

This series of books is designed to help anyone interested in reading better and understanding better the variety of genres in literature.

This book was also written with the wide range of ability levels of third- and fourth-grade students in mind. Both teachers and parents can benefit from the variety of activities provided in this book. A parent can use the book to work with his or her child at home and to help provide a better understanding of a particular genre. Similarly, a teacher can select pages that provide additional explanation for the class about fiction. Both parents and teachers will find the book has been divided into several helpful sections:

- ✏ Define and Recognize
- ✏ Vocabulary Development
- ✏ Reading Stategies
- ✏ Writing Skills

- ✏ Grammar Connections
- ✏ Test Practice and Assessment
- ✏ Culminating Projects
- ✏ Graphic Organizers

The practice of reading should be an enjoyable experience for all children. By practicing vital reading skills and by exposing children to a variety of genres, students will have a positive experience as they prepare for a lifetime of reading.

Meeting Standards

Each lesson in *Discovering Genres: Fiction, Grades 3 and 4* meets one or more of the following standards, which are used with permission from McREL. (Copyright 2000 McREL, Midcontinent Research for Education and Learning. Telephone: 303-337-0990. Website: *www.mcrel.org.*)

Language Arts Standards	Page Numbers
• Uses reading skills and strategies to understand a variety of literary passages and texts	5–7, 11–12, 21, 24–27, 30–34, 39–45, 47, 50, 65–67, 100, 102–106, 111, 113–115, 117, 120–121
• Understands similarities and differences within and among literary works from various genre and culture (e.g., settings, character types, events, point of view, role of natural phenomena)	8–10, 13–15, 17–19, 22–23, 35–36, 46, 48–49, 51–54, 56–58, 60–64, 74–75, 101,107, 110, 112, 119, 129, 130
• Uses the general skills and strategies of the writing process	16, 28–29, 37–38, 55, 68–73, 78, 116, 118, 122–125, 128, 131, 133–135, 137, 140–142
• Uses prewriting strategies to plan written work (e.g., uses graphic organizers, story-maps, and webs; groups related ideas; takes notes; brainstorms ideas; organizes information according to type and purpose of writing)	59, 76–77, 79, 109–109, 126–127, 132, 136, 138–139, 143–167
• Uses grammatical and mechanical conventions in written compositions.	20, 80–99

What Is Fiction?

Fiction is writing that uses imagination. When an author writes fiction, he can write about anything he wants. How fun it is to write fiction! If the writer wants to tell about a mouse that lives in a mushroom, he can. If a writer wants to write about flying to the moon, he can. Of course, people have been to the moon before, but a fiction writer will add things to the story that are not true—that is what makes the story fiction. Fiction can have true events in it, but it does not have to follow true events as they really happened.

Directions: Read each statement. Fill in the circle next to the answer that is correct about fiction.

1. (a) Fiction is writing that is filled with just facts.

   (b) Fiction is writing that is filled with imaginary things.

2. (a) A fiction author can write about anything.

   (b) A fiction author can only write about true or real events.

3. (a) A fiction story cannot have any true events in it.

   (b) A fiction story can have some true events in it.

4. (a) People who enjoy reading about imaginary things will enjoy reading fiction.

   (b) People who enjoy reading only real or true stories will like reading fiction.

5. (a) A true story about the life and habits of a brown bear would probably be found in a fiction book.

   (b) An imaginary story about the life and habits of a brown bear that could fly might be found in a fiction book.

Defining Fiction

Fiction is a style or type of writing. Fiction is different than nonfiction. Nonfiction is based on things that are true. Fiction may have something in the story that is true, but it must also have something in the story that is not true. An author may write a book about snakes. The book is nonfiction if all the information in the book is true. An author might also write a fiction book about snakes. The book may have some facts about snakes that are true, but the book may also have a snake who can talk. Having something made-up or make-believe would make the book fictional.

Directions: Read each sentence. If the sentence is nonfiction, color the snake in front of the sentence *red*. If the sentence is fiction, color the snake *green*.

 1. Snakes do not have arms or legs.

 2. Some people are afraid of snakes.

 3. You can go to the zoo to see a talking snake.

 4. The snakes at the zoo can also sing.

 5. There are many different types of snakes.

 6. Snakes come in different colors.

 7. Some snakes grow up to be college professors.

 8. Some snakes even drive green cars.

 9. Many snakes love playing baseball.

 10. Some snakes are very poisonous.

Judging by the Cover

Sometimes it's hard to know what a story is going to be about just by looking at the cover. A good reader will look carefully inside to see what's "underneath" the cover before deciding to dig in!

Directions: Find four different books. On each book below, write down a different book's title and its author. Then, on the lines provided, explain how you know the book is fiction or nonfiction.

1.

2.

3.

4.

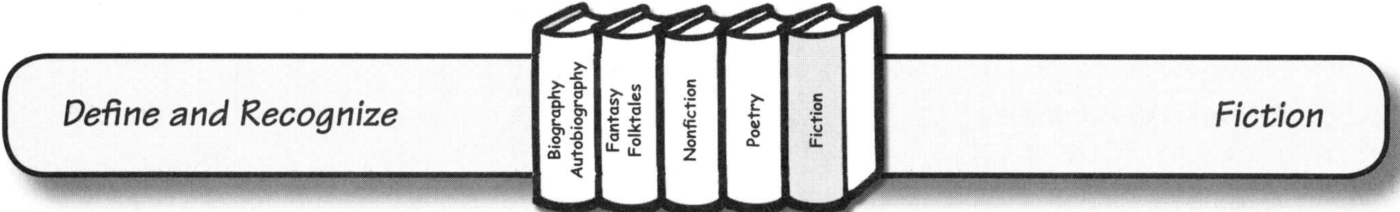

Fiction or Not?

Some books are fiction stories. A fiction story will have something that is not true or that is pretend in the story.

Directions: Look at each set of shapes below. The statement written inside the circle is a nonfiction statement. Change the underlined word to write a fiction statement that is similar to the first sentence. Write your new fiction statement inside the rectangle.

Example: A <u>bird</u> was flying in the blue sky. ➔ A <u>cow</u> was flying in the blue sky.

By changing the word *bird* to *cow*, you have created a fiction statement.

The <u>teacher</u> was teaching the class.

1.

My <u>sister</u> sang a song.

2.

I rode my <u>bicycle</u> to school.

3.

I jumped over the <u>puddle</u>.

4.

Something Extra: On the back of this paper, write a short paragraph. Be sure to use one of your new sentences in your paragraph.

The Many Kinds

Fiction is a type of writing. A fiction story will have something imaginary or pretend in the story. There are many types of fiction stories. Mysteries, science fiction, folk tales, legends, and fairy tales are all examples of fiction stories. Can you think of any other types of stories that might be fiction?

Directions: Look at each picture. Each picture could be a character found in a fiction story. Write a fiction statement to go with each picture.

Example: *I can see everything from up here on my magic carpet!*

1.

2.

3.

4.

Is It Fiction?

Fiction writing is writing that can have many imaginary things in the story. It is the opposite of nonfiction, which is based on fact. For example, a fiction story may be set in a school just like a nonfiction story could be. However, the teacher in the school may be able to turn all of her students invisible whenever she twitches her nose. Or the teacher might be a normal teacher but simply a character the author has created. Having something in a story that is not real is what separates fiction from nonfiction writing.

Directions: Read each statement. If the statement is *fiction*, write **F** on the line. If the statement is *nonfiction*, write **N** on the line.

__________ **1.** The United States of America has 50 states.

__________ **2.** California is part of the United States of America.

__________ **3.** The flag of the United States is red, white, and purple.

__________ **4.** All people who live in the state of Maine have sisters who live in Ohio.

__________ **5.** Most children in America have pen pals from Venus.

__________ **6.** Florida is a great place to visit because the sharks all sing and dance.

__________ **7.** New York is the name of a state.

__________ **8.** When it snows in Nevada, the snow is pink.

Now It's Your Turn: Write one nonfiction and one fiction statement about the place where you live.

Fiction: ____

____

____

Nonfiction: ____

____

____

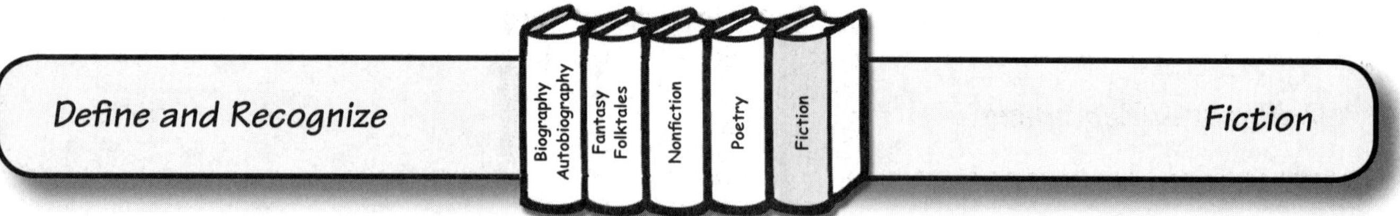

Learn About Fiction

When you read a story, can you tell if it is fiction? Well, first you need to know what fiction is to be able to recognize it. Fiction is writing that allows the author to use his or her imagination. A fiction story can have things in it that are true, but it will also have things in it that are pretend.

Directions: Read each statement. If the statement is fiction, color the shape that it is written in. If the statement is not fiction, draw a big **X** over the shape.

Helpful Hint: The fiction statements below will all be things that can't really happen!

1.

A magical elf grants a wish.

2.

A turtle has a shell.

3.

Monday is a day of the week.

4.

The little girl flew like a bird.

5.

The boy's dog spoke to him.

6.

The mother made pancakes.

7.

The young girl rode her unicorn to school

8.

Blue is a color.

Something Extra: Now it is your turn. Write a fiction statement and a nonfiction statement of your own. Give your sentences to a friend and see if he or she can guess which one is the fiction statement.

Like a Needle in a Haystack

Fiction is writing where the author gets to really use his or her imagination. In nonfiction writing, everything the author puts in the story must be based on fact.

Directions: Below are several haystacks. See if you can find the fiction statements hidden under some of the haystacks. If you find a fiction statement, color the haystack *yellow*. If the haystack does not have a fiction statement, color the haystack *green*.

1. 

An apple is a fruit.

2. 

A carrot is a vegetable.

3. 

Apples grow on peach trees.

4. 

You can grow vegetables in a garden.

5. 

The tomatoes said, "Water me, please!"

6. 

Scarecrows scare away birds.

7. 

If you find the perfect strawberry, you get three wishes.

8. 

Fairies take care of gardens at night.

9. 

Fruits and vegetables are nutritious to eat.

True or False?

There are many types of stories. One type of story is fiction. Fiction is writing that can have characters who exist only in the author's imagination. The settings, too, may also be the author's creation. Really, anything can happen in a fiction story.

Fiction is different from nonfiction. In nonfiction writing, the author must base his story on facts or things that are true. He can write a story about dogs, but he cannot have the dog go on a magical journey or talk to his owner.

Directions: Read each sentence. Fill in the **True** box if the sentence is true. Fill in the **False** box if the sentence is false.

| True | False | 1. There is only one type of story. |

| True | False | 2. Fiction stories have imaginary characters, settings, or events. |

| True | False | 3. In a fiction story, anything can happen. |

| True | False | 4. An author does not use his imagination when writing fiction. |

| True | False | 5. Nonfiction and fiction are the same. |

| True | False | 6. Nonfiction writing is based on facts. |

| True | False | 7. Fiction is always better than nonfiction. |

| True | False | 8. Nonfiction is the best choice for a reader if he wants to read something that is imaginary or pretend. |

Drawing Fiction

A fiction story is a story that has imaginary elements in the story. There may be some true things in the story, but the story must have something in it that is not true. For example, you may read a story about a circus. There is, of course, such a thing as a circus. But in a fiction story, the circus may be a circus the author created using his imagination, or the story may have characters at the circus that have unusual powers.

Directions: See if you can draw some fiction instead of writing fiction. Draw a picture of the ordinary, everyday object listed—but add some details to change the word into a fictional character. Color your picture when you are finished drawing.

Example: a tree 

1. a dog	**2.** a book
3. an apple	**4.** a person

Finding Fiction in the Library

There are many types of books at the library. The librarian can help you find just the type of book you want to read. One section that is in most libraries is the fiction section. The fiction section has many different types of fiction books. Fiction books are stories that have something make-believe or pretend in the story. There are many different styles of fiction. Some people like to read mysteries. Others like to read science fiction. Some like to read fantasies. All of these are types of fiction. The main difference between the fiction books and the nonfiction books is the author's imagination. Nonfiction books must rely on facts or things that are true. Fiction books can have things in the story that are true, but the author also gets to use her imagination and add any pretend things she wants to the story.

Directions: With the help of the librarian or teacher, complete the questions below.

1. Does the library have a section just for the fiction books? _______________________

2. If yes, have you ever checked out a book from this section? _______________________

3. Find two fiction books in the library that you might like to read. Write down the title of each book and the author's name.

    A. Title: ____

    Author's name: _______________________________________

    B. Title: ____

    Author's name: _______________________________________

4. What is the best fiction book you have ever read? _______________________

   ____

5. Why did you like this book? _______________________________________

   ____

   ____

Recognize by Writing It

Have you ever met a cat that could sing or a dog that could fly? Well, you may have met one of these unusual creatures in a book. Fiction books are filled with imaginary people, places, or things. A writer can change an event, a character, a time, or a place to help create fiction.

While some fictional characters have unusual powers or do unusual things, others do not. A fiction author will often write about characters and events that could be real—if he weren't making them up! Some fictional characters look and act just like real people.

Directions: In the space below, write a short fiction story. When you are finished, explain why the story you wrote is fiction.

Story

This story is fiction because ____

____

Character and Setting

A fiction story is made up of many parts. Two important parts of a fiction story are the setting and the characters.

✎ *Setting* is where and when the story takes place.

✎ *Characters* are the people or things that are in the story.

In a fiction story, the setting may be a real place or even a real time from the past or present. But unlike a nonfiction story, a fiction story can also happen in the future.

Although a fiction story can have some things that are true or not pretend, the story itself is created by the author. The story is straight from his or her imagination.

Directions: Pretend you are going to write a fiction story. Think about the story you might write—but don't write it, just think about it. Then answer the questions below.

1. Who are the main, or most important, characters in your fiction story?

   ____

2. Choose one of the characters you listed and describe him or her. What does he/she/it look like? What is his/her/its personality like? _______________________

   ____

3. In the space to the right, draw the character you described.

4. Where and when is the setting of your story?

   ____

   ____

   ____

   ____

Plot It Out

All fiction stories have plot. What is plot? *Plot* is the series of events in a story. It is the problem in the story and then the solution. Every story has a problem that must be solved. If there were no problems, there would be no story.

To understand plot better, think about the familiar story of the three little pigs. The series of events includes the wolf going from door to door trying to eat the pigs. He destroys the first two pigs' homes and ends up at the third home, which is made of bricks. The solution for the pigs is that the third home is so strong that the wolf cannot break it down and instead of the pigs being eaten, the wolf loses out!

Directions: Read the following story. Answer the questions that follow.

The Big Game

Coach R was the best soccer coach. Every practice he would say to us the same thing, and we would try to listen. But at some practices we were not very good. Coach R never gave up on us. "Girls, it is all about the basics. We win as a team; we lose as a team."

We all smiled. Coach R really believed in us. When we were on the field, we did what the coach said. Trap. Control. Pass. Dribble. Shoot. That is the way he wanted it done. Today was no different. We all wanted to win the game. It was the last game of the year. We wanted the trophy.

The sun was shining and we were getting hot, but we were there to play soccer. Our team went on the field to play soccer. "Trap. Control. Pass. Dribble. Shoot. Shoot. Shoot." We shot. We scored. Our team listened, and we won! It was a great day. Coach R is the best coach a team could have!

Directions: On the back of this page, write down the plot of the story, "The Big Game." Remember, plot is the problem and the solution. What problem did the soccer team have? How did the team solve the problem?

What Is What?

Fiction is writing that is not true or real. Fiction is the opposite of nonfiction.
Nonfiction is writing that is about true or real things.

Fiction writing can include many different types of books. Mysteries, science fiction,
historical fiction, fantasy, fables, and fairy tales are all examples of fiction writing.

Directions: Use a dictionary to help you match each word to its definition. Write the
letter of the correct definition on the line.

________ 1. | **nonfiction** | **a.** writing that is based on facts from the past but has some pretend or imaginary items in the story

________ 2. | **fiction** | **b.** fiction writing that teaches the reader a lesson or moral

________ 3. | **historical fiction** | **c.** writing that is true

________ 4. | **fable** | **d.** fiction writing that has imaginary things that may one day come true but have not yet

________ 5. | **science fiction** | **e.** writing that is not true; there are many types of this kind of writing

Learning Suffixes

A *suffix* is a group of letters that is added to the end of a word to form a new word. The letters *tion*—which are seen at the end of the word *fiction*—form a common suffix added to many words.

Part I

Directions: Add the suffix *tion* to the word bases below to create a new word. Write the new word on the line below.

Helpful Hint: You may have to change the spelling of the root or main word to make the new word.

Root Word	Word Base		Suffix		New Word
1. create	crea	+	tion	=	__________
2. evolve	evolu	+	tion	=	__________
3. revolve	revolu	+	tion	=	__________
4. solve	solu	+	tion	=	__________

Part II

Directions: Chose any two of the new words above. Use each word in a sentence of your own.

1. ____

____

2. ____

____

Know What You Read

When you read something that is not true, you have just read fiction writing. Fiction writing is writing that has imaginary characters, setting, or plot. Fiction writing can have some real characters or settings, but overall, most of what is in the story is based on the author's imagination.

When you read fiction, there are often clue words or phrases that help you know if what you are reading is fiction or nonfiction.

Directions: Look at the words below. Decide if what is written would more likely be found in fiction or nonfiction writing.

✎ If it would be found in *fiction*, draw a **star** in the box beside the number.

✎ If it would be found in *nonfiction*, draw a **heart** in the box beside the number.

1. "Once upon a time . . ."

2. "This is a fact."

3. "This is a true story."

4. "This is the true story of the president's childhood."

5. "Once a fairy godmother granted three wishes."

6. "The fairy met the dragon at the restaurant."

7. "Long ago in a kingdom far away. . . ."

8. "These are the facts."

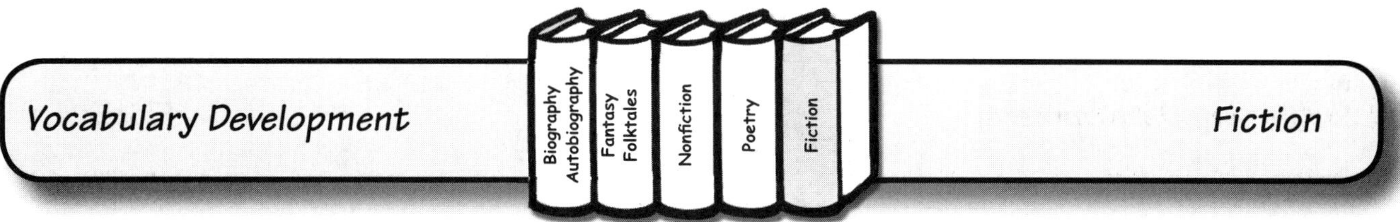

Look It Up

Directions: Answer each question. Use a dictionary or other book for help, if needed.

1. Write down the definition for the word *fiction*.

   ____

   ____

2. What is nonfiction?

   ____

   ____

3. How is fiction different from nonfiction?

   ____

   ____

4. Which do you read more, fiction or nonfiction?

   ____

   ____

   Why do you think you read this type of book more?

   ____

   ____

5. What does the prefix *non* in the word *nonfiction* mean?

   ____

   ____

Know the Language

Fiction is a genre of writing. A genre is a type or style of writing. If a story is fiction, it means the author has added something make-believe or pretend in the story. Fiction writing has many different types of stories. Some of the different types of fiction stories are mystery, suspense, adventure, fantasy, fairy tales, folklore, and historical fiction.

Directions: Use a dictionary to help you learn about the different types of fiction. Look up each word below and write down the definition. Ask your librarian or teacher for help.

1. Mystery ➡ ______________________________________

____

2. Suspense ➡ ______________________________________

____

3. Adventure ➡ ______________________________________

____

4. Fantasy ➡ ______________________________________

____

5. Fairy tale ➡ ______________________________________

____

6. Folklore ➡ ______________________________________

____

7. Historical ➡ ______________________________________

____

Comprehension

Directions: Read the fiction story below. Answer the questions that follow.

The Dancing Red Shoes

Irene was nervous about her dance recital. She would be dancing in front of so many people! The night before the recital she had a dream about dancing. When she woke up the next morning, she couldn't wait to tell her mother about her dream.

"Mother, I dreamed I had a magical pair of dancing shoes," Irene told her mother.

"How were the shoes magical?" her mother asked.

"When I wore my shoes, I didn't make any mistakes," Irene explained. "They were like magic for my feet!"

"Well, you aren't going to believe this, Irene," her mother began, "but your costume just arrived this morning. Look at your new shoes!"

Irene smiled when her mother showed her the new shoes. They were red. Irene now had red dancing shoes. Somehow she just knew she would do great at the recital!

1. Why is Irene nervous? ____

2. Whom does Irene want to tell about her dream? _______________________

3. How does the dream make Irene feel? _________________________________

   ____

4. What arrives at Irene's house? _______________________________________

5. Why does Irene smile when she sees her new costume?

   ____

   ____

Understanding What Is Read

Directions: Read the following story. Check for understanding by filling in the circle next to the correct answer for the questions that follow.

Cleaning Fun

Jenny never said that she had the neatest room in the world. But one day she couldn't even find her socks. They were buried under piles of books, toys, and clothing.

"Let's have a Great Sock Hunt," her mother said. They hunted through the piles. The clothes went into a basket, the books went onto the shelves, and the toys went into the toy box. All the socks were greeted with cheers and awarded points.

"I won!" Jenny cried at last. "I found six pairs! What's my prize?"

"A clean room," said her mother.

1. What was Jenny trying to find?

   (a) her homework   (b) her socks

2. Why couldn't Jenny find what she was looking for?

   (a) She wasn't trying hard enough.

   (b) Her room was too messy.

3. Why did Jenny have fun cleaning her room?

   (a) because her mother made it into a game

   (b) because Jenny loved to clean

4. What lesson might be learned from this story?

   (a) Your room is more fun when it is messy.

   (b) When your room is clean, it is easier to find what you need.

5. Another good title for this story might be _________________.

   (a) "The Terrible Day"   (b) "The Great Sock Hunt"

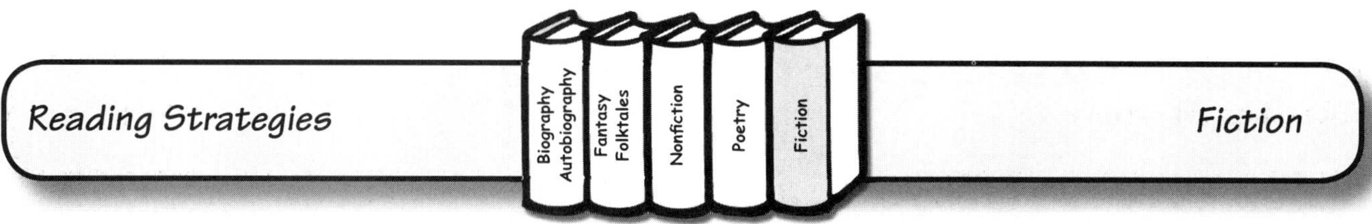

More with Comprehension

Directions: Read the story. Then answer the questions that follow. Fill in the circle next to each correct answer.

Smiles

"Smile," said the woman with the camera.

Teddy didn't feel like smiling. He was sad because his puppy was lost. The woman with the camera took his picture anyway.

"Next," she said.

Teddy jumped off the stool, and his friend Harriet climbed up. The woman with the camera was taking pictures of everybody in Mr. Jenkins's class. Teddy waited until Harriet was done. They walked outdoors.

"What's that?" asked Harriet, pointing toward the sidewalk.

"Curly!" cried Teddy. His puppy had followed him to school! Teddy couldn't stop smiling for the rest of the day.

---

1. Why didn't Teddy feel like smiling for his school picture?

    (a) He had just been to the dentist.

    (b) His dog was missing.

2. Why was everyone getting his or her picture taken?

    (a) It was picture day at Teddy's school.

    (b) Pictures were being taken for a newspaper article.

3. Why was Teddy's dog at school?

    (a) Teddy's dog wanted to learn to read and write.

    (b) Teddy's dog had followed him to school.

4. Another good title for this story might be _______________.

    (a) "Teddy's Bad Day"   (b) "Teddy's Bad Dog"

Think About the Story

Directions: Read the following story. Then answer the questions below.

Mike the Cat

Mike the cat was an ordinary cat. He had two ears, four paws, and a short, stubby tail. Wait a minute! All the other cats that Mike had seen had long tails. Some tails were fluffy, and some were not. But they were all long. Mike decided his short tail would never do. He had to get a long tail! But how?

Mike traveled far and wide, trying to find a long tail. Along the way, he spoke with many cats that had long tails. "My, what an unusual cat you are," they would say. "We have never seen a cat with a short, stubby tail." The cats would gather around Mike, asking all sorts of questions about what it was like to have a short tail. Mike often found himself talking into the wee hours of the morning, telling stories of how he could sleep in front of warm fireplaces without having to worry whether someone was going to step on his tail. Or about the times that he slipped out the back door and spent sunny afternoons chasing squirrels, when the slamming door would have caught other cats by the tail. It wasn't long before Mike became something of a celebrity! Other cats came to him to hear his amazing stories.

Soon, Mike forgot that he had left home in search of a long tail! Maybe being a cat with a short, stubby tail wasn't so bad. Because of his unique quality, Mike had made many friends. "I guess being one of a kind is not so bad after all," Mike thought. "I think I'll keep my short, stubby tail."

Directions: Answer each question.

1. How was Mike different from other cats? _______________________________________

2. Why did Mike's feelings about his tail change over the course of the story?

____

3. What do you think the main point of this story is? What could it teach you?

____

____

The Order of the Story

A fiction story is filled with imaginary or pretend things. However, many things in a fiction story can and have happened. A story may be set in a school building that the author knows about, but the people in the school may all be characters from the author's imagination.

Directions: Read the fiction story below. Then complete the activity that follows.

The Little Prank

Brett was supposed to be watching his baby brother, but he couldn't find him anywhere! He started by searching the house and calling his brother's name. Then he heard giggling.

He went into his brother's room and saw a small bundle hidden underneath the covers.

"There you are!" Brett cried as he pulled the covers away from his brother. His brother laughed at his own joke. Brett laughed, too. The two brothers then spent the afternoon playing hide-and-seek. The little prank turned into a great game.

What happened at the beginning of the story? _______________________________________

____

____

What happened in the middle of the story? ____

____

____

What happened at the end of the story? ____

____

____

Knowing When It Happens

One important strategy for reading a fiction story is understanding the plot. The plot of a story is the series of events in the story. Plot includes the problem in the story and the solution to the problem, or how the problem gets solved.

Directions: Use a story you already know to help you understand plot. Here are some suggestions if you are having trouble thinking of one of your own:

- ✎ "Goldilocks and the Three Bears"
- ✎ "The Three Little Pigs"
- ✎ "Jack and the Beanstalk"

Next, write down the beginning, middle, and end of the story to show you understand the plot.

Story title: ____

What happens at the beginning of the story? ___________________

____

____

____

What happens next? _______________________________________

____

____

____

How does the story end? ____________________________________

____

____

____

Using Pictures to Comprehend

Some fiction stories have pictures with the story. Think about the stories you read in school. Many of these stories have illustrations or pictures to go with each page of the story. Pictures often help give clues to the reader about what is going on or happening in the story.

Directions: Look at the pictures below and write what you think is happening in each picture.

1. 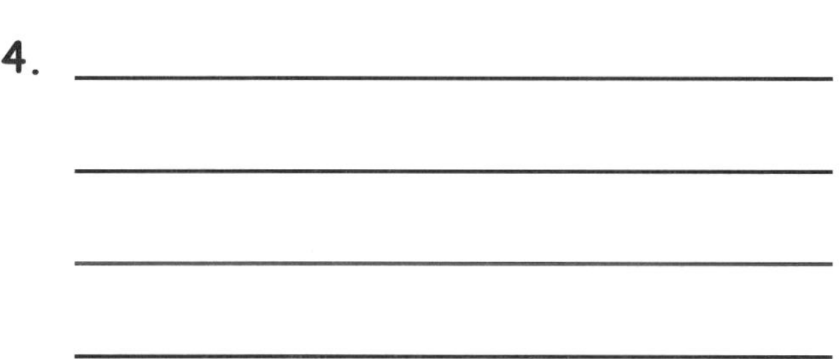

2.

3.

4.

Clues from a Picture

Directions: Look at the picture below. Answer the questions that follow.

1. Could this picture be an illustration for a fiction story? _______________________

   How do you know? ____

   ____

2. Is the woman in this story a good character or an evil character? What makes you guess this? ____

   ____

3. Do you think the animals in the picture are afraid of the woman? Why or why not?

   ____

   ____

4. This picture probably goes with the following story type:

   (a) fiction story   **(c)** biography

   (b) nonfiction story   **(d)** autobiography

Just For Fun: Color the picture above.

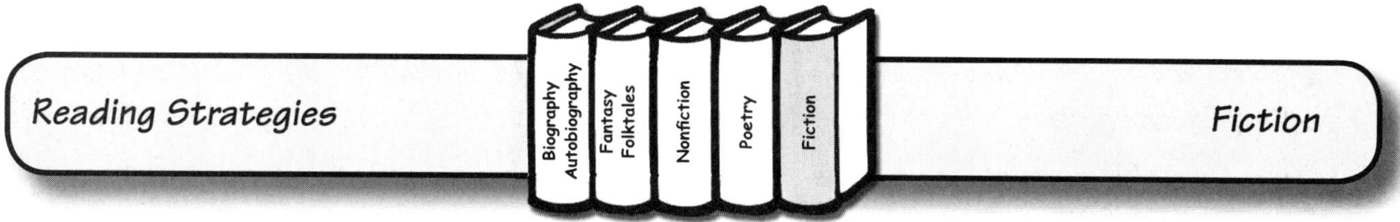

Character Clues

When you read a fiction story, you will find clues about the characters throughout the story. Sometimes the author does not want to just tell the reader a character is a really bad character or a really good character. He will leave clues in his writing so that the reader can figure out for himself that the character is not very nice or is one of the nicest people in the story.

Directions: Read each statement and see if you can guess which word would best describe each character. Then fill in the circle next to the correct answer.

1. When the man saw the stray cat outside his door, he took it inside and gave it a warm bowl of milk and a dish full of tuna.

   This character can best be described as ________________________________.

   (a) selfish   (c) kind

   (b) brave   (d) mean

2. After getting more candy for her birthday than she could ever eat, the young girl looked at her brothers and sisters and screamed, "You can't have any of my candy! It's mine, mine, mine!"

   This character can best be described as ________________________________.

   (a) selfish   (c) shy

   (b) brave   (d) silly

3. The girl wanted to go out on the stage and sing her song. She was almost ready to go when she saw how many people were sitting in the crowd. She just couldn't do it. There was no way she could sing her song in front of so many people!

   This character can best be described as ________________________________.

   (a) brave   (c) kind

   (b) smart   (d) shy

Something Extra: Choose one of the characters above and draw a picture of him or her on the back of this paper. See if your classmates can use picture clues to guess which character you have drawn.

Reading for Character Traits

Directions: Read the following story. Then complete the statements below by filling in the circles next to the correct answers.

Growing Things

It was a sunny day, and Terrell was digging in his garden. He had a special box just for tomatoes, but right now he was watering his sunflowers. They were very tall, taller than Terrell. Each sunflower had bright yellow petals. The sunflowers grew straight to the sky, except for one. That sunflower leaned over the fence as if to talk to Terrell's dog, Duncan.

Duncan barked at the sunflower, but the sunflower didn't answer. Duncan's barking made Terrell laugh. Duncan barked again and then sat down. Terrell put down his watering can and opened the gate for Duncan.

"Okay, okay, Duncan," he said. "The flower won't talk to you, but I will. Time to play."

Duncan wagged his tail in happiness.

Directions: Answer each question. Fill in the circle next to the correct answer.

1. After reading the story, you can tell that Terrell ________________________ .

   (a) enjoys gardening   (b) enjoys being indoors

2. Terrell probably ________________________________ .

   (a) likes animals   (b) doesn't like to be around animals

3. Some hints in the story help us know Terrell probably has a good sense of ________.

   (a) direction   (b) humor

4. Duncan is most likely a dog that ________________________ .

   (a) likes to explore outside   (b) likes to stay inside the house

More with Character

When you read a fiction story, you learn a lot about the characters and how they react in certain situations. Read the story below to learn more about characters.

Directions: Read the story, then answer the questions that follow.

The Birthday

Sadie was very sad. She wanted a new kitten for her birthday gift, but her parents told her she was not going to get one.

"Sadie, we know you want a kitten very much," her mother had explained only the day before. "But a kitten is a lot of responsibility. Right now, Daddy and I think you are too young."

And now it was her birthday. She wanted to be happy on her birthday. She tried to understand what her parents were saying, but in her heart she wanted a pet so much. She already knew that she would name it Cuddles because she planned to cuddle and love it all the time. She guessed she could save the name for the kitten she would get someday when she was older.

At the party, Sadie had opened all her gifts but one. Her parents told her to follow them into the back yard. There, sitting on the porch with a bow around its neck, was a beautiful black kitten.

"Oh, it's Cuddles!" Sadie squealed with delight as she held tight to her new gift. "But I thought you said I wasn't old enough for a pet?"

Her mom and dad grinned at her. "That was yesterday, Sadie. You are another year older today—and definitely old enough to take care of your gift!"

---

1. How did Sadie react when her parents told her she wouldn't get her pet kitten?

____

2. Do you think Sadie will take good care of her pet? How do you know?

____

3. How do you know Sadie is happy about her gift?

____

Understanding Setting

A fiction story can have any setting because it does not have to be based on fact or things that are real. The story can be set in any place or any time. One popular type of fiction is fantasy. In a fantasy story, the writer may tell about a world that is behind a mirror or on another planet. There are no limits to where the story can take place.

Directions: Draw a picture to show each setting that is described.

1. This story takes place on another planet. It is set in the future. People from Earth have moved to Venus to live.	**2.** This story takes place underneath a little girl's bed. There is a village of dust bunnies living in a shoebox underneath the bed.
3. This story take place inside a genie's bottle. A genie has been trapped in the bottle for over 100 years!	**4.** This story takes place in the ocean. There are several young fish who are getting ready for their first day of school.

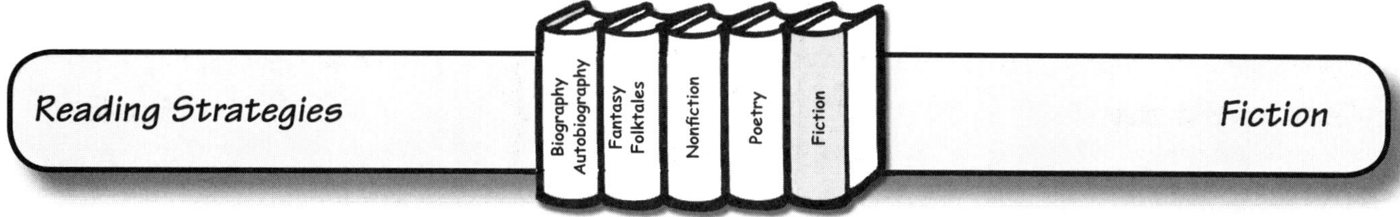

Compare and Contrast

Sometimes a reader will like a certain fiction story because there is something familiar about a character. The character may remind him of his best friend or even himself.

Directions: Read the short story. Then complete the compare-and-contrast chart below. In the left column of the chart, write down all of the ways you are like the main character in the story. In the right column, write all of the ways you are different from him.

The Pitch

Gage couldn't believe how things were going. His baseball team was winning the game. Gage had pitched the last three innings. Now all he needed to do was strike out one more batter and the Hawks would win the game.

The next batter got up and Gage got ready to throw. "Oh no," Gage said to himself. The next batter was his best friend and neighbor, Bobby Taylor.

Bobby grinned at Gage when he stepped up to the plate. Gage knew Bobby was going to try his hardest to hit the ball, but Gage also knew Bobby wouldn't be mad at him, no matter how the game turned out.

It didn't take long for Gage to throw the winning pitch. When the umpire said, "Strike three," everyone on Gage's team was celebrating. Gage walked over to his friend and shook his hand.

Gage watched Bobby walk over to his own team. Gage was glad his team had won, but he still wished he hadn't struck out his best friend.

Compare Ways You Are Like Gage	Contrast Ways You Are Different Than Gage

Summing Up the Story

Have you ever read a really good book and wanted to tell someone about it? You do not tell the person the entire story, do you? Of course not—that would take too long. Instead, you sum up the story or describe it in a few words. Learning how to summarize a story is an important reading strategy.

Directions: Summarize each item listed.

1. Write a summary about your favorite book or movie.

   Title: ____

   Summary: ____

   ____

   ____

   ____

   ____

   ____

2. Write a summary about your day yesterday. (Do not include anything too personal.)

   Summary: ____

   ____

   ____

   ____

   ____

   ____

   ____

Using Great Vocabulary

Directions: Decide what word would go best in each blank. Be sure to use only nouns in the blanks. Then complete the story. Share your completed story with your classmates and see how similar or different your stories sound.

The Unfinished Story

Once upon a ________________________________ there was a princess named

________________________________ and she was kind to everyone she met. One day,

an ugly ____________________________ came hopping into town. He went to the

beautiful princess and said, "If you will give me a ____________________________ .

I will turn into a handsome ____________________________ . The princess decided

to do as he asked. Then the ____________________________ and the

____________________________ lived happily ever after in a castle by the sea.

Making Predictions

Part I

Directions: Read the following story. Make a prediction about how you think the story will end. Use the lines below to write an ending to the story.

Fight

"Fight! Fight! Fight!" yelled the kids.

The kids on the playground looked like ants running everywhere. Two boys were in the center fighting. They were punching each other. They were throwing fists. Both boys were saying bad words and calling each other bad names.

It did not look good. I did not want to get in the middle of that fight. A boy pushed me as I stood in the circle. I fell into one of the boys who was fighting. He punched me in the head.

"That hurt!" I yelled. "Stop it! I don't want to fight with you. Let go of me!"

Now both boys were punching me. One hit my head. The other punched me in the stomach. It was not a good day at all. I did not want to fight. Why was I in the middle of a war?

Mr. Jones came out of the lunchroom. He opened the door and gave the "dirty look." We all stopped. I stared. My arms had bruises on them. The kids were all pointing to me. It was a nightmare.

____

____

____

____

____

Making Predictions

Part II

Directions: Now read the original ending for the story. Answer the questions that follow.

Fight *(cont.)*

Lucky for me, my mom came to wake me up in a few minutes. She pulled my pillow and touched my nose. I was still asleep when I said, "Do not punch me again. I might get a bloody nose!"

---

1. Which ending do you like better, your ending or the original ending? Why?

____

____

____

2. How is your new ending different from the story's original ending?

____

____

____

3. Do you think the main character in the story would normally be the type of student to get into fights at school? How do you know?

____

____

____

Predictable You

Readers often use clues from their reading to guess what is going to happen next in a story. This type of guessing is called making a prediction. When the reader predicts what is going to happen, he makes the guess based on what he already knows about the story. For example, pretend you have a best friend who loves chocolate. Someone offers your friend a piece of chocolate cake. Based on what you already know about your friend, you would most likely predict she would take the piece of cake. However, if you knew your friend was trying to lose weight, you might predict she would say "no, thank you" to the person offering her the cake.

Directions: Use what you know about yourself and make a prediction about how you would react in each situation. Then write your answer.

1. You are spending the night with a group of your friends. Someone in the group suggests telling scary stories. Someone turns off the light to make it even scarier. Your friend's mother suggests that anyone who doesn't want to hear scary stories should come and join her for a movie and popcorn.

   What would you do? ____

   ____

   ____

2. Your teacher is planning a party. She needs volunteers to stay after school and help decorate. There is going to be a lot of work involved, and you heard from last year's class that the party really was not much fun. Your teacher comes to you and asks for your help with the party. She says she has already talked to your family, and it is okay with them if you stay and help.

   What would you do? ____

   ____

Predict What Will Happen

It can be especially fun to make a guess in a mystery story. The reader might guess who committed the crime or who is the guilty character. But really, it is fun to predict no matter what type of story it is!

Directions: Below are some familiar stories. Read each familiar story, then see if you can make a prediction about what would happen if some of the events were changed.

1. Goldilocks entered the cabin of the three little bears. She tried the porridge, but one bowl was too hot, one bowl was too cold, and one bowl was just right. She went and sat down to eat her bowl of porridge, then in walked the three bears.

   What might happen next? ____

   ____

   ____

   ____

   ____

2. Jack spent the money his mother gave him for food on some magical beans. He planted the beans, and a stalk grew all the way up through the clouds. Jack climbed up the stalk to another world. While he was up in the clouds, someone came by and chopped down the beanstalk.

   What might happen next? ____

   ____

   ____

   ____

   ____

Recognizing Historical Fiction

Historical fiction is writing that is based on some historical information, but the story itself is made up. The author of historical fiction must do research to make sure the historical parts are accurate. The rest of the story is all up to the writer's imagination.

Directions: Read the following historical fiction story and answer the questions below.

Henry Learns to Fly

Henry was lying down in the grass. He did not want anyone to see him. The grass was tall, so he was safe.

Two brothers were working not far away. They were making something that looked funny. It had two wheels. One was in the front. The other was in the back.

"Hey, Orville, could you help me with this?" asked Wilbur.

The boys worked and worked. They put something on top of the wheels. The boys got on, and it started to move. It went faster and faster.

Henry yelled, "What are you two doing?"

"We are trying to fly," they said.

"Can I learn how to fly, too?" he asked.

"Maybe," they said.

Henry went home and asked his mother. She said, "Yes." Henry watched and waited.

In 1903, Orville and Wilbur made something that had a motor, and it also had wings. It was made of cloth. It was made of wood.

Orville got inside of it. Wilbur smiled. They started the engine. It moved into the air. It stayed in the air for 12 seconds.

Henry yelled, "Now, that is flying!"

1. Who are the two historical people mentioned in this story? _______________________

2. What did these two people do? ____

3. How do you know the story is historical fiction?________________________________

____

More with Historical Fiction

Story Page

Historical fiction is a fiction story that also includes historical facts in the story. Some of the characters in the story might have even been real people in history, but the story itself is from the author's imagination.

Directions: Read the historical fiction story below. Then complete the "Questions Page" that goes with the story (page 46).

The Soldier

Mary Ann and her mother were taking food to the soldiers in the Continental Army. Mary Ann's parents wanted to see the colonies break away from England and become a separate nation. Mary Ann's own father was off fighting in the war, and she did not know when she would see him again. Mary Ann was glad to help in any way she could.

At the camp she saw one man sitting off by himself. He reminded Mary Ann of her father. He was very tall and seemed very kind when he smiled at her.

"Sir, can I offer you something to eat?" Mary Ann asked the soldier.

"Thank you, but no. Please, save your food for my men. They need the food more than I do," the man said.

Mary Ann then realized this was no ordinary soldier. He was a leader, and the other soldiers were his men.

"You could do a kindness for me, though," the stranger said as he handed Mary Ann a letter. "Can you see that this letter is delivered to my wife? It would mean a great deal to me."

"Of course, sir," Mary Ann said as she took the letter. She was glad she could do something for the soldier with the gentle smile and kind eyes.

When she left the camp, she looked down at the letter and saw a familiar name. She could not believe it! She had just met General George Washington!

More with Historical Fiction

Questions Page

Directions: Read each question. Fill in the circle next to the correct answer.

1. Where was Mary Ann going with her mother?

   (a) to take food to the soldiers   (b) to go shopping for clothes

2. Mary Ann's father was ________________.

   (a) at the camp where they were taking the food

   (b) off fighting in the war

3. The soldier did not want the food Mary Ann offered because ________________.

   (a) he didn't like the food

   (b) he wanted her to give the food to the other soldiers

4. Mary Ann realized the soldier was ________________.

   (a) George Washington   (b) Abraham Lincoln

5. You can tell this story is historical fiction because ________________.

   (a) real events and people from history are mentioned in the story

   (b) the story takes place during a war

6. Mary Ann was able to help the soldier by ________________.

   (a) agreeing to deliver his letter   (b) helping him write his letter

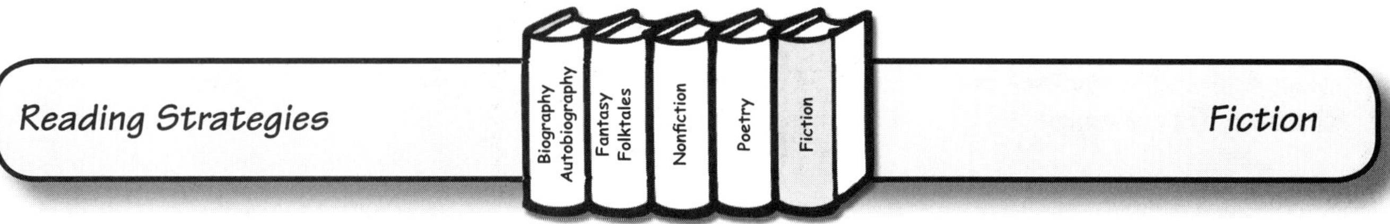

Fantastic Fiction

There are many types of fiction stories. One type of fiction story is fantasy. Fantasy stories are filled with make-believe or pretend. Unicorns, dragons, and fairies are all examples of characters that might appear in a fantasy story. In a fantasy fiction story, anything is possible; nothing is impossible.

Directions: Read each story description. If the story sounds like a fantasy story, color the smiley face. If the story description does not sound like fantasy, color the frowning face.

1. The boy fell through the mirror and found himself in another world. No matter how hard he pushed against the mirror, he could not get back to his real world.

2. How excited she was! Today was her birthday, and she just knew she was going to get something really great. Last night her mother had told her she couldn't wait to see her face when she got her birthday present.

3. The young girl was very quiet. She could feel her bed moving. There was something under it. She was almost too scared to look, but she couldn't stop herself. She leaned over the bed and peered into the darkness. Two beady eyes peered back at her.

4. She had always wanted a horse. She couldn't believe she finally had one! This beautiful creature seemed to belong to her. She had never had a horse; she had certainly never had a unicorn. She wondered what the unicorn would eat or where it would sleep. But even more than that, she wondered if the unicorn planned to stay.

Something Extra: Choose one of the story parts above. On the back of this page, use it to help you write a story of your own.

Comprehending Fantasy

Fantasy is fiction writing that is filled with make-believe or pretend. Anything can happen in a fantasy story—and often, it does!

Directions: Read the story below and answer the questions that follow.

Wishes

Have you ever wanted to have someone else's feet? Sounds silly, huh? But I have. My sister has tiny feet, and my feet are huge! My sister wears a tiny, cute shoe size, but I wear a large, gigantic shoe size. And so I have just always wished for my sister's feet. Last night when I saw a shooting star in the sky, I made a wish. I wished I didn't have such large feet. I wished that I could have little feet just like my sister's feet.

The next morning when I went to put on my shoes, they did not fit. My feet slipped right in and right back out. What was wrong with me?

I looked at the shoes. They were mine. I tried again. Too big. In fact, they looked like clown shoes. Maybe it was the laces. I tied the laces tighter. No use. The shoes were still too big.

I heard a scream from my sister's room. I ran to her room. Jessie was staring at her feet. They were huge. She was looking at her shoes.

"I got monster feet last night! My shoes don't fit."

I looked at my feet. I looked at Jessie's feet. An idea came to me. I ran to my bedroom and got my shoes. She gave me her shoes. We put them on. I didn't want to tell her what had happened. All I can say is that I hope all my other wishes do not come true!

1. What did the girl wish for? ____

2. How do you know her wish came true? _____________________________________

____

3. How did Jessie feel about her new feet? __________________________________

____

Mysterious Fiction

There are many different kinds of fiction stories. One of these is the mystery or suspense story. A fiction story that is full of suspense or mystery can be a lot of fun to read. It is always fun to wonder what is going to happen next in a story.

Directions: Read each situation. If the situation could be from a mystery or suspense story, color the question mark *blue*. If not, color the question mark *red*.

 **1.** Kara's parents had left her alone for the night. She'd locked all the doors—but when she got ready for bed, one of the doors was unlocked!

 **2.** The parade was starting at 10:00. Callie couldn't wait. She was going to be riding a float with her dance class. She had helped the other students work on the float and was very proud of how it had turned out.

 **3.** The first time Scott heard the noise, he didn't think much about it. He was sure it was just the wind. But the second time, he was worried. This time it sounded like the noise was coming from inside the house, and he was supposed to be the only person home.

 **4.** Macey had always wanted to make straight *A*'s. Report cards were coming out in two days. She had an *A* in all of her classes but one. Mr. Carson's class was so hard. Her *A* average in his class depended on a project she had to finish. She just wasn't sure if she could get it done in time.

Reading Mystery and Suspense

Directions: Read the story. Then follow the directions below.

The Case of the Missing Keys

It was time for school. Mom was in the car. The baby was in the car. I was in the car. Dad was not in the car.

He came out of the house. His face was all red. "Have you seen the car keys?" I shook my head. Mom shook her head. The baby shook his head.

"Are you sure you haven't seen the car keys?" Dad asked again.

Mom got out of the car. I got out of the car. I took the baby out of his car seat.

"We'll help you look for the keys," said Mom. "I am sure one of us will find them in the house."

I looked in the bathroom and under Dad's bed. Mom looked in the pockets of his pants and on his desk.

The baby went right to his bed. He picked up his blanket, and he picked up his pillow. He picked up Dad's keys.

"Dad!" I yelled. "The baby had the keys under his pillow!"

"Thanks! Now, let's race to the car so you are not late for school!"

Directions: Draw a **key** on the line beside each statement that is *true* about the story. If the statement is *false*, draw an **X** beside the statement.

__________ **1.** The family couldn't leave because no one could find the car keys.

__________ **2.** The keys were under the pillow.

__________ **3.** The mother had hidden the keys.

__________ **4.** No one could find the missing keys.

__________ **5.** The family was going to the mall.

Reading Realistic Fiction

One type of fiction is realistic fiction. *Realistic fiction* is fiction that could really happen. For example, a story about a student in elementary school could be an example of realistic fiction. The actual school, students, and teachers might all be part of the author's imagination, but the events in the story are things that could actually happen in an elementary school. This makes the story realistic fiction.

Directions: Fill in the circle next to the event that might be found in a realistic fiction story.

1. (a) The boy rode the dragon across the sky, looking for the wicked trolls.

   (b) The boy rode in a plane across the sky, looking at the houses below him.

2. (a) The two friends went to the fair.

   (b) At the fair, the children found a genie in a bottle.

3. (a) The mouse asked the cat not to eat him.

   (b) The cat purred and curled up near the fire.

4. (a) The campers worked hard getting their camp ready.

   (b) The boy could not get the fire started, so he asked the dragon for help.

5. (a) The clouds in the sky were white and fluffy.

   (b) The fairy rested for a while on the top of the cloud.

6. (a) Derek loved eating ice cream.

   (b) The mice were busy planning a party for the princess.

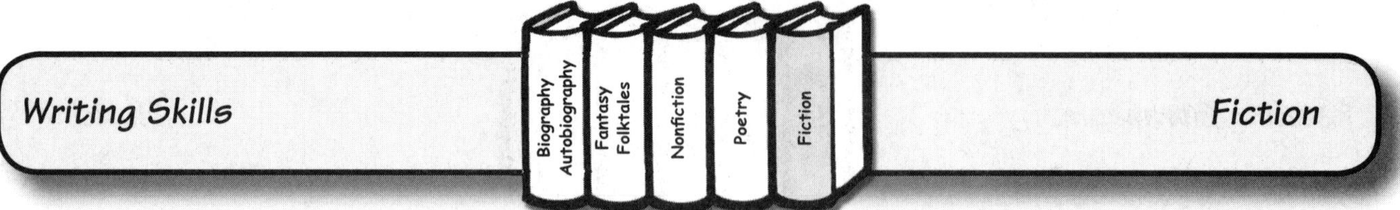

Writing Fiction

Writing a good fiction story takes a lot of work. There are many steps involved in writing a story. The author must decide who the characters will be, where the setting of the story will be, and what the plot of the story will be. You can practice getting started on a story by completing the activity below.

Directions: Imagine you have been asked to write a story about an imaginary world that exists somewhere near your school. Think about the story idea and answer the questions that follow.

1. Where is the setting of your story? How do the characters get to this setting?

____

____

____

____

2. Who are the main characters in your story? Are the characters real people or imaginary creatures or both?

____

____

____

3. What are the main events that will happen in your story? Are there any major problems that must be solved?

____

____

____

____

Just For Fun: Use the information you have gathered and write a fiction story.

Dealing with Plot

Plot is an important part of all fiction stories. The plot is the series of events that happen in the story. It is the problem and then the solution to the problem. Think about some familiar stories and practice writing down the plot.

Directions: Choose three of the stories listed below. Then write down the plot of each story.

> "Jack and the Beanstalk"   "The Three Little Pigs"
>
> "Goldilocks and the Three Bears"   "The Boy Who Cried Wolf"
>
> "Hansel and Gretel"   "Rapunzel"

1. The plot of ____ is

(title of story)

____

____

____

2. The plot of ____ is

(title of story)

____

____

____

3. The plot of ____ is

(title of story)

____

____

____

Understanding Plot

The plot is the series of events that happen in the story. But it is also more than that. It is the problem in the story and the solution to that problem. A story is interesting because there is some problem to be solved. If the prince and the princess of a story immediately fell in love and lived happily ever after, then where is the story?

Directions: Read the story. Answer the questions.

The Rat and the Princess

Mia was a princess who lived in a big, blue castle. Her dad painted purple and yellow flowers on the wall. The halls had green leaves and green carpet. She was spoiled.

"I want to wear my pink dress! I want my purple shoes! Give me my tea set! Where are my dolls?" she yelled.

One day she took her dolls to the garden. They had tea. She dropped her teapot in a hole.

"Who will get my teapot?" she asked.

"I will," said the little rat.

"You are too ugly," she said.

"I will get it anyway," said the rat. "And then, you must take me home with you."

He got the teapot, and the princess went home. She left the rat in the garden.

He followed her home. She did not like him, so she threw him into the pond. Suddenly, he became a prince! The princess saw he was a nice prince, so she married him. They lived happily ever after.

1. Write examples that show Mia was a spoiled princess. ______________________

____

2. Because Mia was spoiled, she did not want to get her own teapot. Who offered to solve her problem? ____

3. At the end of the story, what happens to the rat? ______________________

____

Retelling the Story

The plot of a story is the events that happen. One way to learn about plot is to practice retelling a story. If you watch a movie and someone asks you what the movie was about, then you are telling the plot. When you tell what happened, you are telling the series of events.

Directions: Read the fiction story. Then, in the space below, write the plot of the story.

The Tiny Black Cow

Parker was a tiny black cow. He lived on a big farm, and Katie the cow was his friend. She also lived on the farm.

Spencer lived on the farm, too. He was a white cow with black spots.

Parker did all the work. He got the eggs. At night, he fed the dogs. He made the food. All he did was work.

"I want cookies," said Katie. She sat in her chair.

"I want cake," said Spencer.

Parker worked and worked. He was getting tired of working. His friends were lazy. He made a plan.

One stormy day, he made a big cake. It was chocolate. It had frosting. The cake looked great! All his friends wanted to eat it.

"Not this time," said Parker. "I will eat it myself."

He ate it all by himself. The friends could not have one bite. They were mad.

"You have to help out!" said Parker. "You have to work, too."

Now they all do chores. And they all eat cake!

The plot of "The Tiny Black Cow"

____

____

____

____

Writing the Setting

Every fiction story must have a setting. The *setting* is the time and place a story takes place. A fiction story can take place anywhere and at any time.

Directions: Think about some settings that have occurred in your own life. Describe the setting you were in when the following events occurred:

1. *First day of school:*

____

____

____

____

2. *Yesterday:*

____

____

____

____

3. *Your last birthday:*

____

____

____

____

Something Extra: On the back of this page, draw and color a picture of a setting where you would slike to go for vacation!

Know Your Setting

A fiction story can be set absolutely anywhere and during any time period. Sometimes the author may even have a character travel back in time!

Directions: Read the story and then answer the questions that follow.

A Pilgrim Day

"Em, it's time for bed," called her mom.

Emily turned off her TV and settled under the covers. Her mother turned off the light. But Emily wanted to read for a few minutes. She took out her flashlight and turned it on. The room started to move. It was going in circles!

Emily was wearing a dress. It had an apron on the front. She wore big shoes. They had buckles. Her bed was made out of straw.

"Emily, time to eat," called Ma from down in the kitchen.

Emily went down the ladder.

"Today is the day you have to do all the chores. I have to walk to Grandma's house."

"I know, Ma. In the morning I feed the hens. I get the eggs and sweep the floor. I have to watch baby Liz, too."

"And in the afternoon?" Ma asked.

"Set the table. Fix Pa his dinner. Wash the dishes. Before bed I have to write on my slate. Pa will help me with my letters and numbers."

"Today we will see how big you are. I'm counting on you, Emily!"

"I will do all the chores, Ma. Take good care of Gram. She needs you, too."

---

1. When the story begins, where and when does it take place? __________________

   ____

2. What clues do you have that the story has changed settings? __________________

   ____

3. Does the story change to the future, or does it go back to the past? __________

   How do you know? ____

4. Why do you think the setting in the story changed? ____________________________

   ____

Story Characters

Story characters are the people, animals, or imaginary creatures in a story. The characters are who the story is all about. In a fiction story, the characters can be real people, but they can also be fairies or talking dogs.

Directions: A good writer describes a character so that the reader can easily picture what the character looks like. Write a description of each character listed. Then hand your paper to a friend and see if he or she can draw the characters you have described.

Character	Drawing

1. a good friend

2. a talking rabbit

3. a friendly fairy

4. a scary monster

People You Know

Every story is based around the characters in the story. It is each character's story the reader learns about as he reads. In "Jack and the Beanstalk," the reader learns about Jack's family and how they are very poor. The reader learns Jack believes in magic and how much he wants the magical beans to help his family. The reader also learns how brave Jack is as he faces the giant. Great characters help make great stories.

Directions: Think of a character you know from a book you have read or a book assigned by your teacher. Use this character to help you answer the following questions.

1. What is the character's name? _______________________________________

2. In what book did you first meet this character? _______________________

3. How old do you think the character is? _____________________________

4. Is this character a person or is it something else? If something else, then what is it?

    ____

5. Describe what the character looks like. ______________________________

    ____

6. Can you think of anyone in real life who reminds you of this character? In what ways does the person remind you of the character?

    ____

    ____

7. Is the character someone you would want to be friends with? Why or why not?

    ____

    ____

Creating Imaginary Characters

Fiction writers can have a lot of fun creating the characters in their books. In a fiction book, the characters do not have to be real things or even real people.

Directions: Pretend you are writing a story for a book of fairy tales. You have been asked to create three characters for the story. One character must be able to grant wishes, one character must be able to fly, and one character must be a little boy or girl the same age as you.

Use the space below to describe your characters. Give as much detail about each character as you can.

Character #1: ____

Description: ____

____

____

Character #2: ____

Description: ____

____

____

Character #3: ____

Description: ____

____

____

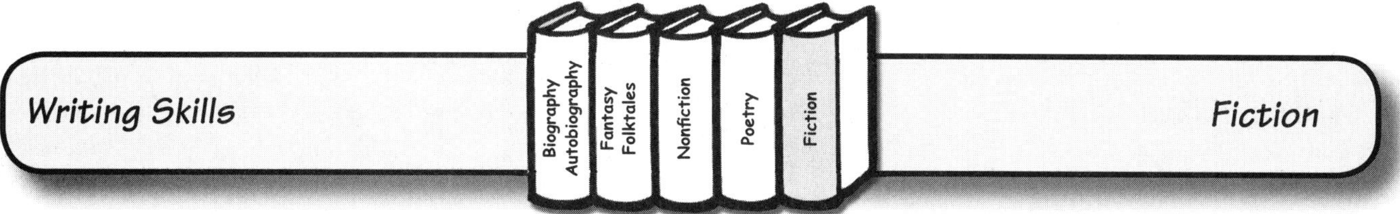

The Traits of the Characters

Every character in a story has special *traits*, or things about him that make the character special. Some characters are mean. Some characters are nice. Some are funny and some are shy. A character can have any trait the writer wants to give him. See what special traits you can give to each character by following the directions below.

Directions: Look at the picture of each character. Then use your best words to describe the character. Be sure to use lots of descriptive words!

Character	Traits/Description
1.	
2.	
3.	

What Type of Character?

Story Page

Directions: Read the story below. Then read and complete the questions on the "Questions Page" (page 63).

The Fawn

Sara and her father planned a hike up a mountain trail near their home. The trail they chose began at the foot of the mountain and led all the way to the top. Sara had packed lunches earlier that morning. Her father filled their backpacks with other supplies, and they were off!

As they started up the trail, Sara's father pointed out many different plants that lined the trail. He showed Sara the difference between the leaves of an aspen tree and the needles of a spruce tree. Sara was glad that her father knew so much! She always learned something whenever they went on a hike.

"Look over there," Sara whispered suddenly. They had just turned a corner on the mountain trail. Lying in the grass next to the trail was a small baby deer, or fawn. It looked at them with wide eyes, but it did not move.

"Where is its mother?" Sara wondered aloud. "Do you think we should stay here and watch it?"

"That's a good idea," answered her dad. "We must not go any closer, though." As they sat down and unpacked their lunch, Sara asked her dad why they couldn't go any closer to the fawn. He explained that sometimes if the mother smelled humans too close to her baby, she would be too afraid to come back. Sara and her father agreed they would not get too close to the fawn.

Soon a larger deer walked slowly up to the fawn nestled in the grass. After a few quick sniffs and a cautious glance at Sara and her father, mother and baby ran quickly down the trail.

Sara and her father packed up their supplies and continued up the mountain. They knew that the fawn was now safe.

What Type of Character?

Questions Page

1. Do Sara and her father like to do things together? _________________

How do you know? ___________________________________

____

2. Give an example to show Sara's dad knows a lot about nature.

____

3. Do you think Sara is a good daughter? Give reasons for your answer.

____

____

4. Would you like to spend time hiking with a good friend or someone in your family? Why or why not? ___________________________________

____

5. Do you think if Sara went hiking with someone other than her father that she would be kind to the creatures in the woods? Explain your answer?

____

____

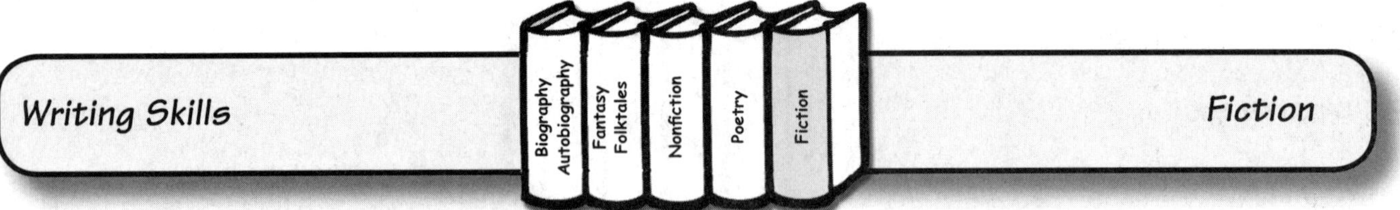

A Rose Would Smell As Sweet

Names are important. Often, characters in books are given names that the author believes fit their personality.

Directions: Imagine you are in charge of renaming everything. Give each character or object below a new name. On the lines below each picture, explain why you chose each new name.

1. New Name	**2.** New Name	**3.** New Name
4. New Name	**5.** New Name	**6.** New Name

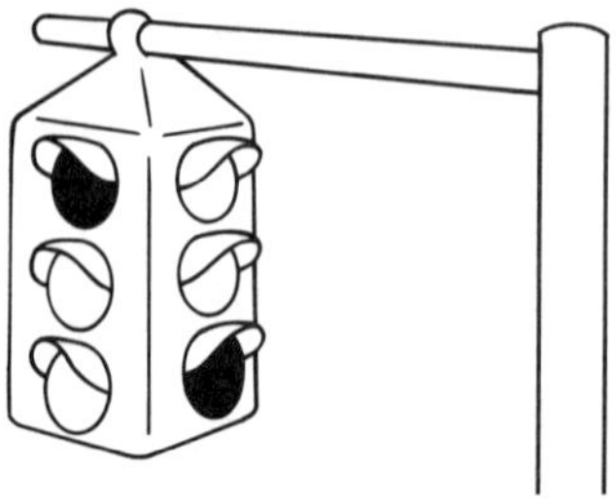

©Teacher Created Resources, Inc.

Describing Characters

Directions: Think about positive character traits that would best describe each character. Then write the traits you think of on the lines provided. Remember to use only positive words to describe each one.

1. a police officer *Trait #1:* _______________ *Trait #2:* _______________ *Trait #3:* _______________	**3.** an astronaut *Trait #1:* _______________ *Trait #2:* _______________ *Trait #3:* _______________
2. a football player *Trait #1:* _______________ *Trait #2:* _______________ *Trait #3:* _______________	**4.** a student *Trait #1:* _______________ *Trait #2:* _______________ *Trait #3:* _______________

Something Extra: What if you were a character in a book? How would someone describe you? Think of three traits that describe you. Write these on the lines provided.

Trait #1: ____

____

Trait #2: ____

____

Trait #3: ____

____

What's the Effect?

One important thing a writer must know about is cause and effect. For example, if a little boy in a story falls in a mud puddle, the author must decide what the effect of this will be. Does the little boy have a mother who will get mad because the little boy is all muddy? Does the little boy have a mother who won't care because the little boy is wearing his play clothes? Think about cause and effect as you answer the questions below.

Directions: Think about a day at school to help you learn about cause and effect. Then read each statement. Write your answers in the boxes provided.

1. If you oversleep for school, an effect might be . . .   →

2. If you forget your lunch or lunch money, an effect might be . . .   →

3. If you make straight A's on your report card, an effect might be . . .   →

4. If you don't get to bed until very late on a school night, the effect might be . . .   →

5. If you don't do your homework, an effect might be . . .   →

6. If you lose your pencil, an effect might be . . .   →

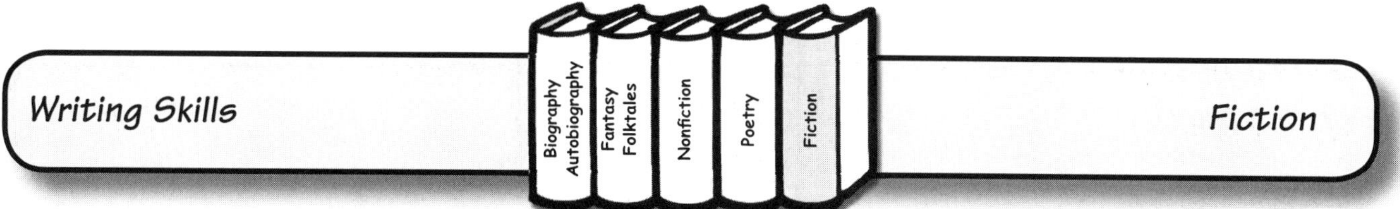

This, Then This

A good writer knows the importance of cause and effect. Cause and effect helps explain why a character behaves a certain way in a story. If a character is afraid of the water and he is invited to a swimming party, the effect may be that he will not go to the party.

Think about cause and effect as you complete the activity below.

Directions: Write your own cause-and-effect relationships.

If this happens . . .   **Then this happens.**

Example:

If I forget to brush my teeth ➡ then I may get cavities.

1. ➡

2. ➡

3. ➡

4. ➡

5. ➡

More Cause and Effect

Story Page

Directions: Read the story below. Answer the questions that follow on page 69.

Fire!

When the fire alarm started to buzz, the class knew what to do. Brittany got in line and whispered to her friend Kelsey, "I wonder why we're having another fire drill. We already had one this week."

All the classes lined up on the playground. Then everyone turned and looked at the school. They were waiting for the "All Clear" bell to ring so that they could go back inside. But instead of the bell, they heard sirens! A huge fire truck raced up to the school. And then another one came. And right behind them were the police!

Everyone started whispering. And then Brittany heard, "Fire! It's a real fire!"

A real fire! Brittany felt very excited and very scared at the same time. Would their class burn down? What about Jason, their pet hamster?

Just then the class heard the "All Clear" bell. The children looked at each other in surprise. Then they started back into the school.

"What happened?" they asked their teacher as soon as they were back inside.

"Oh," said their teacher, "One of the teachers was making toast, and it burned a little. The smoke set off the fire alarm."

Brittany whispered to Kelsey, "I'm glad it wasn't real. But it was exciting!"

More Cause and Effect

Questions Page

1. When the fire alarm started to ring, what was the effect? _________

____

____

2. What caused the fire alarm to ring? _____________________

____

3. What effects did the children worry about because of the alarm?

____

4. Who came to the school because the alarm went off? _________

____

5. What effect did the "All Clear" bell have on the children? ______

____

6. Have you ever had a fire drill at your school? _______________

   If yes, what did you do when the alarm sounded? ___________

____

Fiction or Nonfiction?

In fiction writing, anything can happen. Nonfiction writing is based on what is true. Fiction writing can be based on everyday events, but the characters, setting, and other parts of the story might all be part of the writer's imagination. Nonfiction writing cannot be based on a writer's imagination. It must be able to be proven true.

Directions: Read each nonfiction statement. Rewrite the statement to make it a fiction statement.

Example:

Nonfiction: The horse ate the apple.

Fiction: The horse ate the apple and then flew away.

1. Nonfiction: The child played with the toys.

   Fiction: ____

   ____

2. Nonfiction: We went to school.

   Fiction: ____

   ____

3. Nonfiction: The boy ate his lunch.

   Fiction: ____

   ____

4. Nonfiction: The girl watched the movie.

   Fiction: ____

   ____

5. Nonfiction: The alarm clock made a buzzing sound.

   Fiction: ____

   ____

Real or Not Real?

When reading a fiction story, it is important to understand that what is happening in the story is all part of the author's imagination. Yes, some things in a fiction story can be real. An author could write a story about the first Thanksgiving. He may even include the names of some of the people who were at the first Thanksgiving. But, the story itself would be a fiction story because he does not really know exactly what happened on that day. When an author writes things that are real or true, this is called nonfiction. When an author uses his imagination and creates or adds to a story, this is called fiction.

Directions: Read each fiction statement. Change each fiction statement into a nonfiction statement, or something that is true.

Example:

Fiction: The horse ate the hay and then flew over the barn.

Nonfiction: *The horse ate the hay and then walked over to the barn.*

1. Fiction: The dog asked his owner, "When are you going to feed me?"

   Nonfiction: ____

   ____

2. Fiction: The girl cleaned up her room with a wave of her wand.

   Nonfiction: ____

   ____

3. Fiction: The boy turned invisible so no one would see him.

   Nonfiction: ____

   ____

4. Fiction: She wished for a pizza, and one magically appeared!

   Nonfiction: ____

   ____

Now It's Your Turn: Practice writing fiction. Write a sentence that could not happen in a nonfiction story.

____

Story Starter

Part I

Fiction is writing that is not based on what is real or true. In a fiction story, an author can create characters, settings, and plot. Nonfiction stories must be based on things that really happened. A fiction writer does not have to follow those rules; he can write about absolutely anything!

Directions: Practice being a fiction author. Choose from one of the two story starters below. Cut out your story starter and glue or tape it on Part II of this activity (page 73). Then write an ending to the story. Remember, this is your story, so use your imagination!

Story Starter #1

"Gage, it's time to come in and finish your homework," Gage's mother yelled.

Gage was in his yard. He was playing and having lots of fun. He did not want to come inside and do work. He was pretending to be an explorer. He was hot on the trail of a snow monster. If only he had a few more minutes, he knew he could find it.

Gage got ready to go inside, even though he did not want to. Suddenly, Gage heard a mighty roar. He turned to look behind him.

Story Starter #2

The star was the brightest Jessie had ever seen. She just knew it was a wishing star.

"I wish I could have a puppy," Jessie whispered, looking at the star.

Jessie had wanted a puppy for as long as she could remember. Her parents had always said "no" whenever she asked. They had so many reasons why she couldn't have one that Jessie had just about given up on her wish. But she had often wondered what would happen if a puppy just showed up at her house. Would her parents let her keep it?

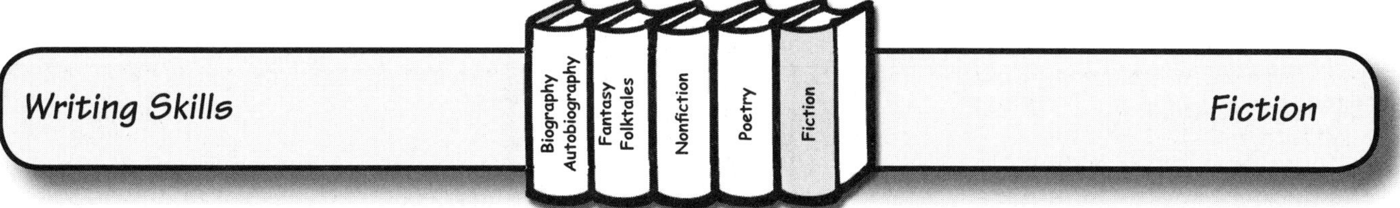

Story Starter

Part II

Directions: Cut out the story starter you chose from Part I of this activity (page 72). Tape or glue the story starter here. Then write an ending. What happens in your story?

Really Fantastic Fiction

In fantasy fiction, magical things can happen. Children can have super powers, unicorns can really exist, and fairies might be found flying around!

Directions: In the space below, write a fantasy fiction story. Be sure to include at least one magical creature as one of your characters.

Something Extra: Draw a picture to show the setting of your fantasy fiction story.

Having Order

A good story must have order to it. There must be a beginning, a middle, and an end. When a writer puts things in a certain order, it is called *sequence*. Practice your sequencing skills by completing the activity below.

Directions: Think about your day so far. Think about the major events that have occurred in your day. Write them in the order they occurred. Decide which events came first, which events came in the middle, and which events came at the end (or to where you are right now!).

Helpful Hint: You do not have to fill in all the lines.

My Day So Far . . .

First, these things happened: _______________________________

____

____

Next, these things happened: _______________________________

____

____

Finally, these things happened: _______________________________

____

____

Here is something that might happen later in the day:

____

____

In Order

Story Page

A good writer must decide the sequence or order of the events in a story. Practice your sequencing skills by doing the activity below.

Directions: Read the story. Answer the questions that follow on page 77.

The Horses and the Troll

Kerry was the oldest horse in the family. He was six years old. He liked to build things. Kerry was small, but he was smart.

Tim was the second oldest brother. He was four. Tim loved to read books. He was strong and tough.

Nate was the baby brother. He was very smart. Nate liked to play games.

Every day, the three brothers loved to eat grass.

One day, the three brothers met a mean troll who owned the bridge. The troll made the brothers pay $1.00 a day to cross the bridge so that they could eat grass on the other side.

One morning, the grass was not good. It tasted sour and dry. The brothers were mad. They wanted to go home early, but the troll stopped them. He wanted to eat them for lunch!

The troll tried to eat Kerry, but Kerry made a boat and crossed to the other side.

The troll wanted to eat Tim, but Tim was too tough to chew. His tail was like rubber.

When Nate came along, the troll tried to eat him, too, but Nate said that they must play a game first. If the troll won, he could eat Nate for lunch. If Nate won, then the three brothers would never have to pay $1.00 each day.

Nate won the game. The three brothers never had to pay the money again!

In Order

Questions Page

1. List the horses from youngest to oldest. ___________________________

____

____

2. List the horses from oldest to youngest. ___________________________

____

____

3. Number these three events in the order they happened in the story. Write a "**1**" next to the event that happened first, a "**2**" next to the event that happened second, and a "**3**" next to the event that happened third.

__________ The troll tried to eat the three horses.

__________ The grass did not taste good.

__________ The horses wanted to go home early.

4. Which horse did the troll try to eat first? ___________________________

5. Which horse did the troll try to eat second? ___________________________

6. Which horse did the troll try to eat last? ___________________________

Just For Fun: On the back of this page, draw and color a picture of the mean old troll and the three horses.

Don't Reverse the Order

When an author sets out to write a story, she must decide in what order she wants the events to take place. She must plan the story before she writes. As a reader, you expect things to happen in a certain order. You would not expect someone to write the ABCs in reverse order. People don't call them the ZYXs, do they?

Use what you know about order and complete the activity below.

Directions: Put the following lists in correct order.

1. Write the days of the week in order:

1. Sunday

2. Write the names of the months in calendar order:

1. January

3. Write the names of the people in your family in alphabetical order:

4. Write the names of the eight planets of our solar system in alphabetical order:

Helpful Hint: The planets are Mercury, Venus, Earth, Mars, Jupiter, Saturn, Uranus, and Neptune.

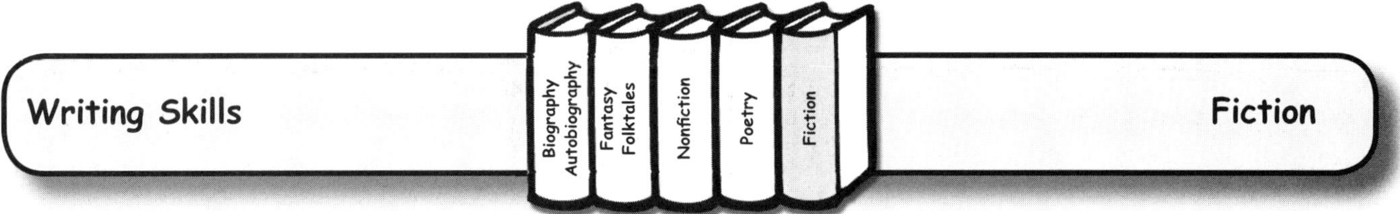

Making More Predictions

When you were a little baby, you did not always understand everything that was going to happen. You had not yet learned to make predictions. If someone gave you a cup of juice, you might turn the cup over to see what would happen to the juice. After doing this several times (and probably getting in trouble several times), you finally learned to predict that if you turned the cup over, the juice would pour out onto the ground. And so, you finally learned not to turn the cup over and lose all of your juice.

Good readers also learn how to make predictions. Good readers look for clues in the writing to help them predict what will happen next in a story.

Directions: Look at the crystal ball. Write inside the crystal ball five predictions or things you believe will happen tomorrow. Then on the following day, go back and see which of your predictions came true. If they did not come true, explain what you think happened to stop your predictions from happening.

What's Inside?

Materials: glue, scissors, paper, and a gift box

Directions: Color each gift box and cut just the dotted lines around each one. Then glue a blank piece of paper to the back of this sheet. Lift up each gift-box section where you have cut it on the dotted lines. Draw a picture there, and then lower the piece of paper to close the box. Write clues underneath each box. Make sure the clues can help someone predict what is inside the box.

Exchange papers with a classmate. See how many clues he or she needs to guess the gift!

1.

Clues

____
____
____
____

2.

Clues

____
____
____
____

3.
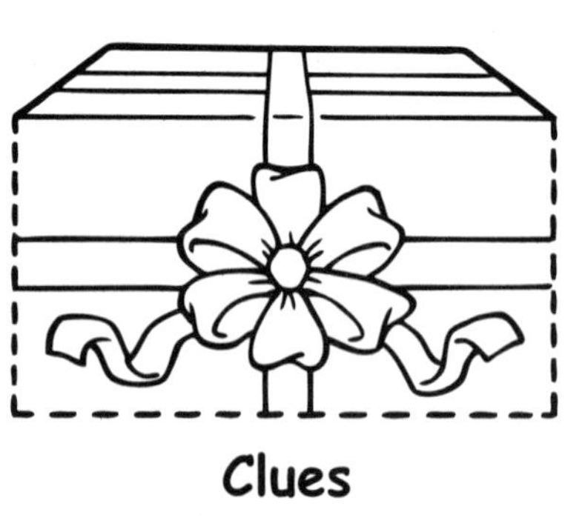

Clues

____
____
____
____

4.
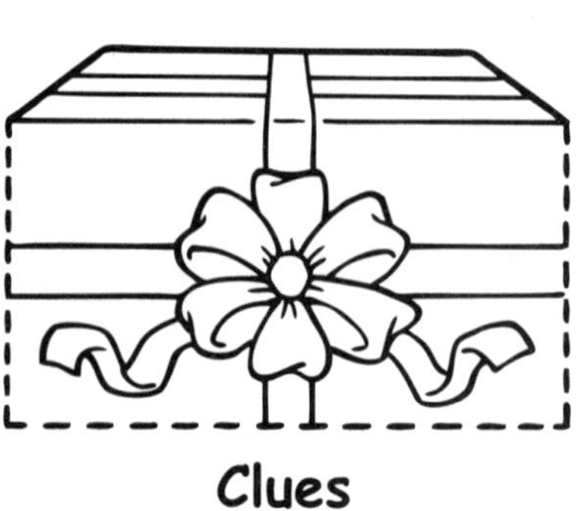

Clues

____
____
____
____

Start on the Right Track

Directions: Read each sentence inside each boxcar. If a sentence has correct capitalization, color the boxcar and cut it out. If the sentence does not have correct capitalization, do not color the boxcar or cut it out.

When you are finished, glue your capitalization train to a separate sheet of paper.

Helpful Hint: Your final train should have six boxcars.

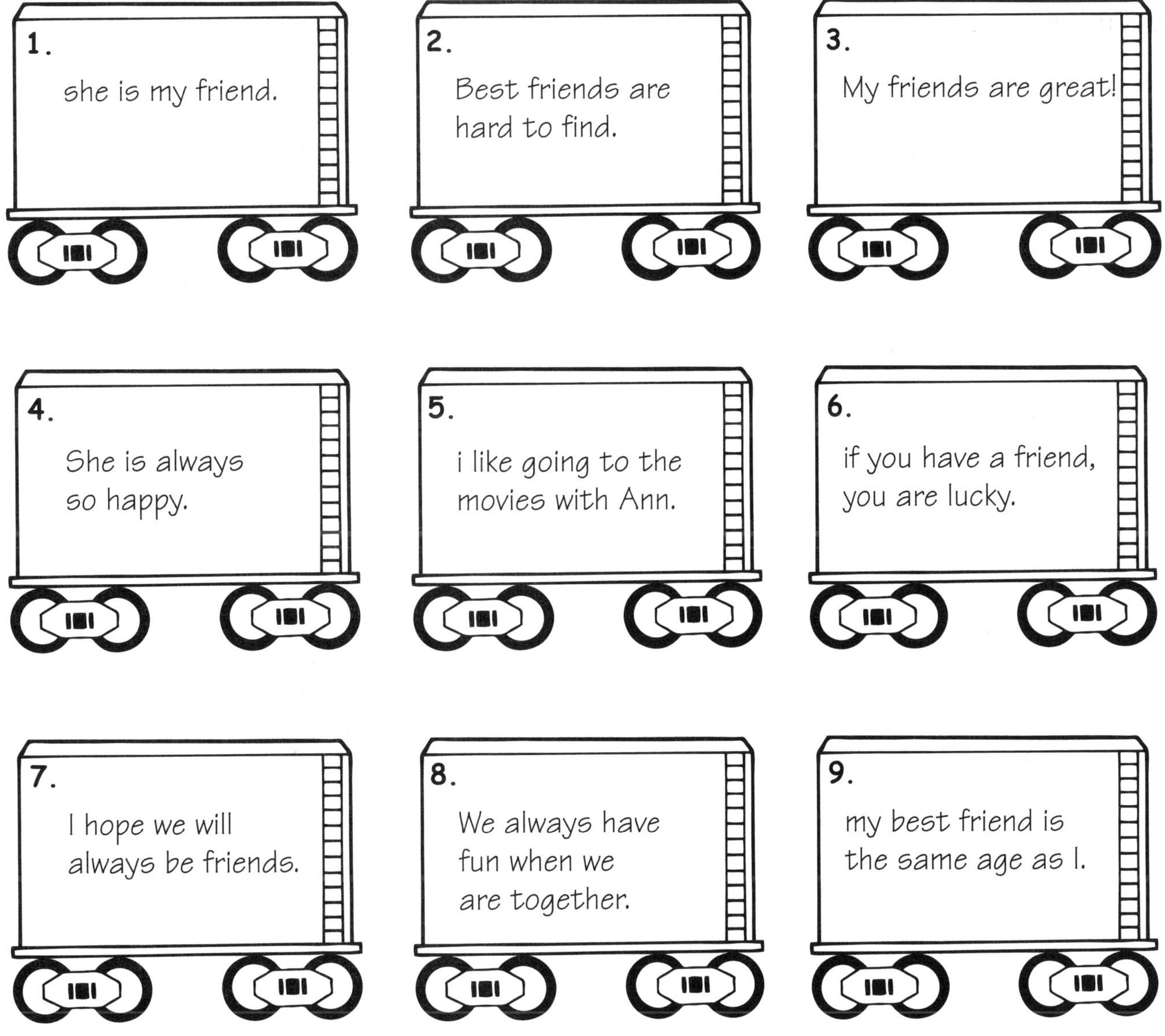

Pulled from a Story

Directions: The following sentences are all pulled from different fiction stories. Read each sentence. If the sentence is capitalized correctly, write the letter **C** on the line provided. If the sentence is incorrect, rewrite the sentence correctly.

______ **1.** Once upon a time, a long time ago, there lived two princesses.

______ **2.** once there was a shaggy, brown dog that liked playing in a large park.

______ **3.** the moon lit up the sky.

______ **4.** princess ayala lived in a rainbow castle.

______ **5.** The stars began to glow brightly.

Fishy Business

A good writer can't have any fishy business in his writing. Not only does his writing have to be interesting, but it must also be correct!

Directions: Help this writer straighten up his work by getting rid of all the sentences that are written incorrectly. Read each sentence inside each fish. If the sentence is written correctly, **color** the fish. If the sentence is written incorrectly, draw an **X** on the fish.

1. catfish have whiskers like cats.

2. Once I caught a turtle instead of a fish.

3. Fish do like worms.

4. Have you ever been fishing?

5. fish cannot live without water.

6. One type of fish is a clown fish.

7. I love to fish.

8. Worms do not like fish.

9. clown fish do not tell jokes.

What About the Endings?

Writers know the ending of something is just as important as the beginning. It is certainly important to know what type of end punctuation to use whenever you are writing.

There are three types of end punctuation:

✎ Use a *period* when you are writing a statement or a mild command.

Example: Princess, please bring me my tea.

✎ Use a *question mark* when asking a question.

Example: Princess, where is my tea?

✎ Use an *exclamation point* when showing excitement or emotion.

Example: Princess, you spilled my tea!

Directions: Rewrite each sentence and add correct end punctuation.

1. Once upon a time there lived two princesses

   ____

2. The two princesses were very good friends

   ____

3. Have you ever had a very best friend

   ____

4. How wonderful it is to have a good friend

   ____

5. The two princesses grew up and married two brothers

   ____

6. What do you think was special about the two brothers

   ____

7. Each of the two brothers was a prince

   ____

8. How amazing that each girl would fall in love with a prince

   ____

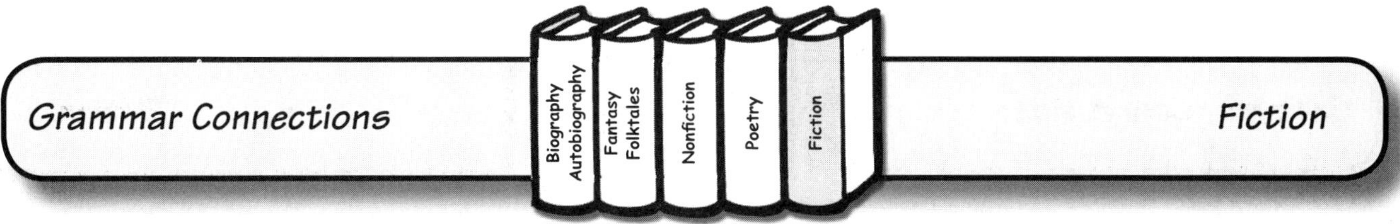

The Important Ending Punctuation

Fiction writing is fun to read, but it would be hard to read if there were no ending punctuation marks. A good writer knows how to use a period, a question mark, and an exclamation point correctly.

Directions: Read the following fiction story. There are 10 ending punctuation mistakes. Circle each mistake and add correct ending punctuation.

The Secret Teller

Once upon a time, there was a bird that lived in a jungle. All of the animals liked to talk to the bird. They thought he was friendly His name was Mr. Parrot. He liked to listen to everyone's secrets Mr. Parrot heard the zebras tell their secrets as they ate the grass. He listened to the elephants as they played in the water. He could easily hear the lions talking He would fly into the trees to hear the giraffes, and he would listen to the deer as they ate.

But do you know what else he did He would tell everything he heard to the monkeys in the trees. How terrible

Telling the monkeys was a bad idea because the monkeys were a bit tricky They did not think it was right for the bird to tell secrets. They wanted to teach the bird a lesson So do you know what the monkeys decided to do They asked the animals for help. The next day, all the animals dressed up as monkeys.

Soon, Mr. Parrot flew near He told the monkeys all the secrets he knew. He whispered all of their secrets. He told every single one.

As the animals heard their secrets, they took off their monkey masks. When Mr. Parrot was finished talking, he saw all of the animals he knew. The next day, no one would talk to him

Mr. Parrot apologized to all of the animals. He asked the animals not to tell him any more secrets. It was too hard for him to keep secrets, he explained.

"Yes," said the monkeys, "be careful of your secrets." And this advice is still good today.

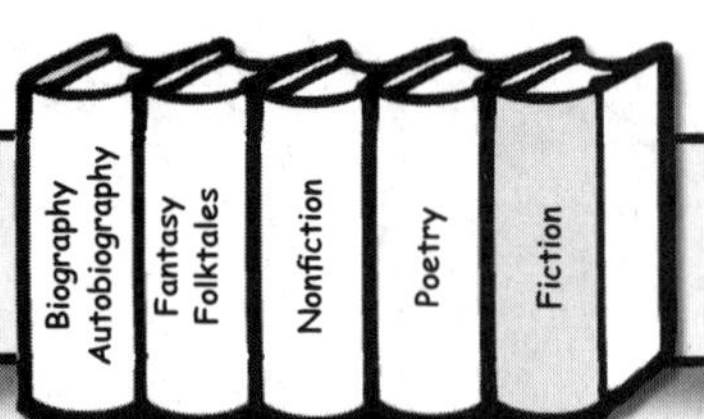

Seeing Things Clearly

A good writer uses lots of descriptive words. *Adjectives* are words that are used to describe nouns. An adjective answers the question "how many," "which one," or "what kind of" about a noun or pronoun.

Directions: Look at the words written inside the stars. Write at least three adjectives that help describe the word.

1. 

____
____
____

4. 

____
____
____

7. 

____
____
____

2. 

____
____
____

5. 

____
____
____

8. 

____
____
____

3. 

____
____
____

6. 

____
____
____

9. 

____
____
____

More with Adjectives

An adjective is a word that helps describe or give more information about a noun or pronoun. Good writers use adjectives so their writing is more descriptive.

Directions: Read the following fiction story below and on page 88. Finish the story by adding adjectives where they are needed.

The Buttons

A **(1)** _____________________ boy named Grant ran into the classroom with

ten buttons in his hand. He was so excited. His teacher had asked everyone

to bring in **(2)** _____________________ buttons from home. They needed the

buttons for a **(3)** _____________________ project.

Grant spent a **(4)** _____________________ time picking his buttons. His mother

had a special **(5)** _____________________ basket. In the basket were many

different buttons. There were small buttons and **(6)** _____________________

buttons. There were simple buttons and **(7)** _____________________ buttons.

There were even smooth buttons and **(8)** _____________________ buttons.

Grant dumped all the buttons onto the floor. He liked the sound they made

as they fell out of the basket. He wanted to see each button. The little

buttons that came off his Dad's shirts, he did not like. He liked the

(9) _____________________ buttons from his mother's sweaters. He

took his time picking just the right ones for school.

More with Adjectives *(cont.)*

The Buttons *(cont.)*

Soon it was time for the **(10)** ______________________ project, and the teacher told everyone to take out his or her buttons.

Grant proudly placed each of his buttons on his desk. The teacher came around the room and took the buttons. She placed them in a bag and shook them up. Then she gave every child 10 different buttons. Grant ended up with all **(11)** ______________________ buttons, just like the little buttons that came off of his Dad's shirts.

In the end, Grant did not think the project was so **(12)** ______________________ .
In fact, Grand did not like the project at all. He just wanted his buttons back!

Something Extra: Make a list of eight things you can do with buttons.

1. ____

2. ____

3. ____

4. ____

5. ____

6. ____

7. ____

8. ____

Who or What It's About

The characters in a fiction book are very important. The characters are whom the story is all about. They are the subjects of the story. Sentences also have subjects. The subject of a sentence is who or what the sentence is all about.

Example: The princess escaped from the dragon.

The princess is the subject of the sentence. She is the one who escaped.

Directions: Read over each sentence below. Rewrite each sentence and then circle the subject of each sentence.

1. Kristen wanted to bake a cake.

   ____

2. The cake was going to be strawberry.

   ____

3. Kristen was baking the cake for her sister's birthday.

   ____

4. Allison was turning six.

   ____

5. Their parents had bought the gifts.

   ____

6. Kristen was in charge of the cake and the decorations.

   ____

7. Balloons were hung inside the house.

   ____

8. Allison loved her presents and hcr strawberry cake.

   ____

A Verb in Action

A fiction story is filled with action verbs. *Action verbs* are words that show the action in a story. Words like *kick, jump, hop, smile, laugh,* and *scream* are all examples of action verbs. These words help the characters in a story come to life!

Part I

Directions: Think about words that show action. List as many action verbs as you can think of on the lines below.

____________________   ____________________   ____________________

____________________   ____________________   ____________________

____________________   ____________________   ____________________

Part II

Directions: Choose any five of the verbs you listed above. Write a short story using the five verbs. Circle the five verbs as you use them in your story. Use the back of the page if you need more space.

My Story

Piecing It Together

Puzzle Pieces

All sentences have a subject and a verb. The *subject* is who or what the sentence is all about. The *verb* usually shows the action in the sentence, or it sometimes links the subject to something on the other side of the sentence.

Examples: I ate the pizza. (The subject is *I*, and the verb is *ate*.)

The pizza is delicious. (*Pizza* is the subject, and *is* is the verb. The verb links the subject to the word *delicious*.)

Directions: Look at each puzzle piece. Match any five subject puzzle pieces with any five verb puzzle pieces. Then on the "Subject and Verb Match" sheet (page 92) write your matches and create five sentences using your matched pieces.

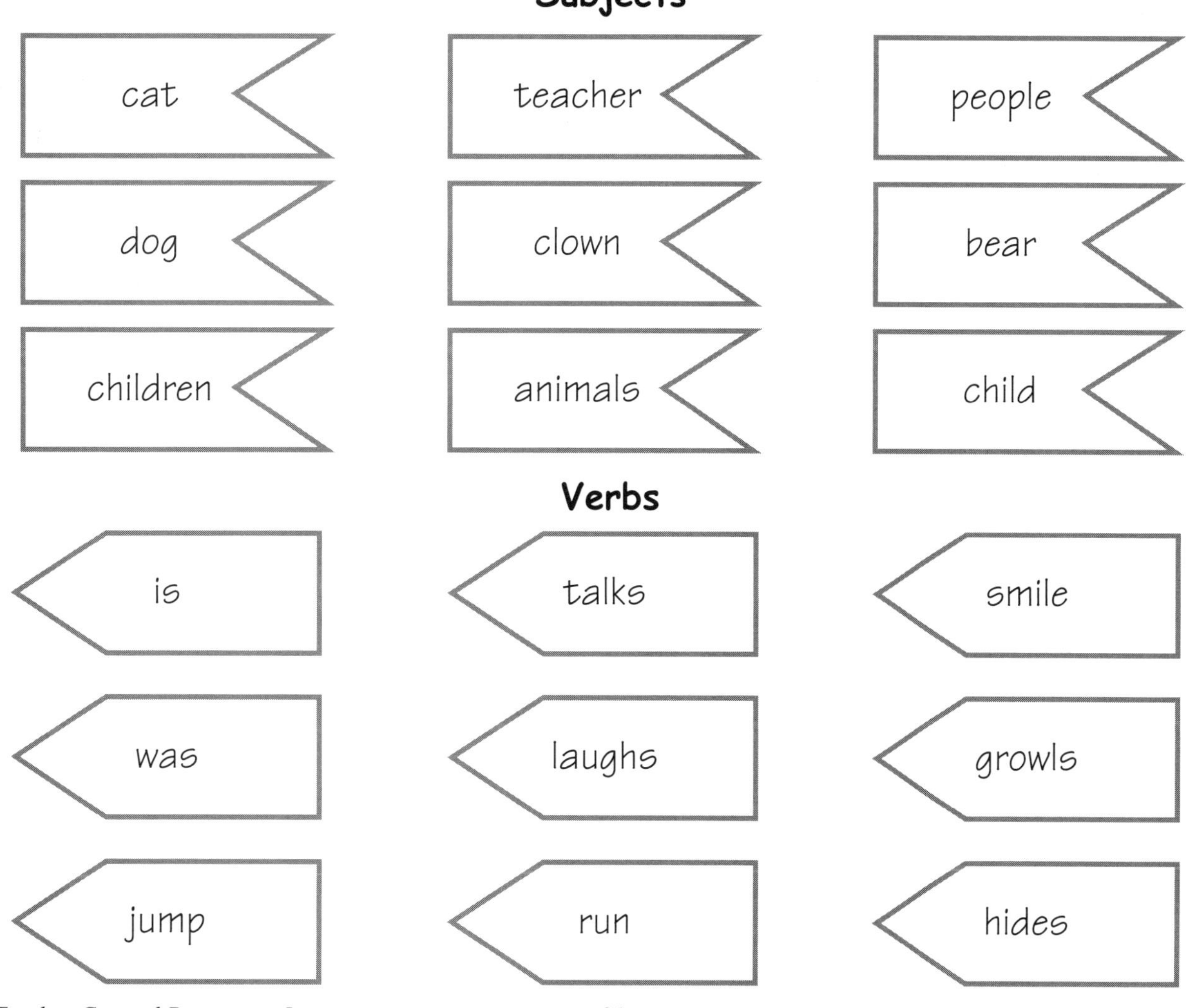

Piecing It Together

Subject and Verb Match

1.

| Subject | Verb |

Sentence: ____

2.

| Subject | Verb |

Sentence: ____

3.

| Subject | Verb |

Sentence: ____

4.

| Subject | Verb |

Sentence: ____

5.

| Subject | Verb |

Sentence: ____

Important Spelling

All authors know the importance of good spelling. Good spelling makes a story easier to read. When something is easier to read, it is easier to understand. All writers must carefully proofread their writing to check for spelling mistakes.

Directions: Proofread the following fiction story. Correct any spelling mistakes you find by circling the misspelled word and then writing it correctly on the lines below.

Wunce there was a shaggy, brown dogg. The dog liked to play in a neighborhood parkk. The brown dog learned to be friendly to new anumals. The dog learned the lesson when she saw a new butterfly at the park. The purtty butterfly was sadly watching everyone play. But the butterfly was not playing. So, the dog asked the butterflie to play.

The butterfly waz so happy! Twoday the shaggy, brown dog and the beautiful butterfly are best friends.

Correctly Spelled Words

1. ______________________________

2. ______________________________

3. ______________________________

4. ______________________________

5. ______________________________

6. ______________________________

7. ______________________________

8. ______________________________

Watch What You Type

A computer is a wonderful thing. Many errors can be found when typing on a computer. But a good writer knows a computer cannot catch every mistake. Good writers still must know the rules of their language.

Directions: Look at the sentences below. Find the mistakes the computer could not find. Circle each mistake and rewrite the sentence correctly.

1. The dog got fir all over the couch.

   ____

   ____

2. A daisy is my favorite flour.

   ____

   ____

3. If you want to go faster, just petal harder.

   ____

   ____

4. I flew home on a plain.

   ____

   ____

5. We had ate guests for supper.

   ____

   ____

6. We did all of this four you!

   ____

   ____

More of the Same

A writer must be very careful about the words he uses in his story. One mistake made by beginning writers is to easily confuse words that sound the same but have different spellings.

Example: That is a delicious bury. (*incorrect*)

That is a delicious berry. (*correct*)

The words *berry* and *bury* are *homophones,* words that have the same sound but different spellings and different meanings. A good writer must be careful to always choose the correct word when writing so that the reader doesn't become confused.

Directions: Read each word. Write a word that sounds just like the word listed but is spelled differently and has a different meaning. Be prepared to explain what each word means.

Example: ruff ______rough______

1. blew ________________
2. write ________________
3. hi ________________
4. bee ________________
5. stake ________________

6. sale ________________
7. tic ________________
8. sent ________________
9. daze ________________
10. dye ________________

Challenge: colonel ________________________________

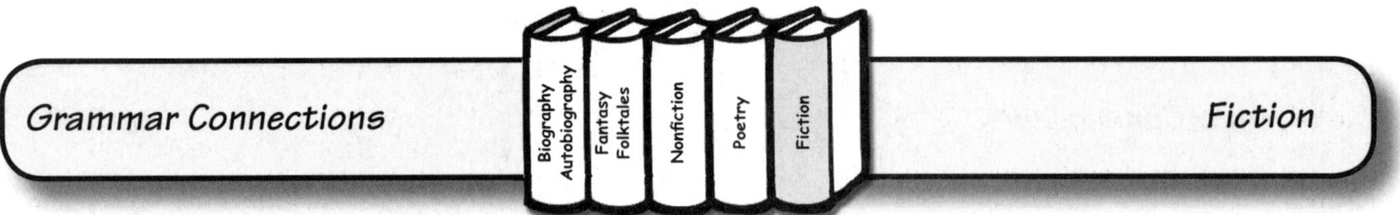

Commas in a Series

Commas are an important type of punctuation. Commas are often used in writing to separate items in a series. The series might be single things or it might be a series of events. Good writers use commas to make their writing easily understood.

Example: I love apples, oranges, and grapes.

I love to go to the movies, go to the pool, and go on vacations.

Directions: Read each sentence. Add commas wherever they are needed.

1. Goldilocks went to the house opened the door and sat down at the table.

2. There were three bowls of porridge three spoons and three glasses.

3. She tried the porridge from one bowl tried the porridge from the second bowl and tried the porridge from the third bowl.

4. The porridge in the three bowls was too hot too cold and just right.

5. After the meal Goldilocks was full tired and sleepy.

6. She left the kitchen climbed the stairs and went into the bedroom.

7. She tried the first bed the second bed and the third bed.

8. The mattresses on the bed were hard soft and just right.

9. Goldilocks lay down closed her eyes and went to sleep.

10. Suddenly the door opened, and Father Bear Mother Bear and Baby Bear entered the room.

11. Imagine their surprise to see that someone had eaten their porridge someone had been in their house and someone was still there!

12. Goldilocks woke up screamed and ran out of the house.

Commas for Listing

Commas are used when a writer wants to list three or more things. The comma helps separate the items in a series.

Example: She has visited the states of Alabama, Kentucky, and Tennessee.

Directions: Answer the questions below in complete sentences. Use commas as needed.

1. What are three of your favorite fiction stories? _______________________________

____

2. Who are three of your favorite fairy-tale characters? _______________________________

____

3. What are three subjects you learn about in school? _______________________________

____

4. List three things you wish you could have. _______________________________

____

5. Give three reasons why you should not have to do homework. _______________________

____

6. List three reasons why you should have to do homework. _______________________

____

Finding Commas in Fiction

Commas are used throughout the writing of fiction books. The main use of a comma is to show a pause. It is a helpful reminder to the reader to slow down. Once you start looking for commas, you will be surprised to find you see them almost everywhere.

Directions: Choose any fiction book. Look through the book and find five sentences that have commas in them. Rewrite the sentences on the lines below. Circle the place(s) in each sentence where the comma(s) is/are located.

1. ____

____

____

2. ____

____

____

3. ____

____

____

4. ____

____

____

5. ____

____

____

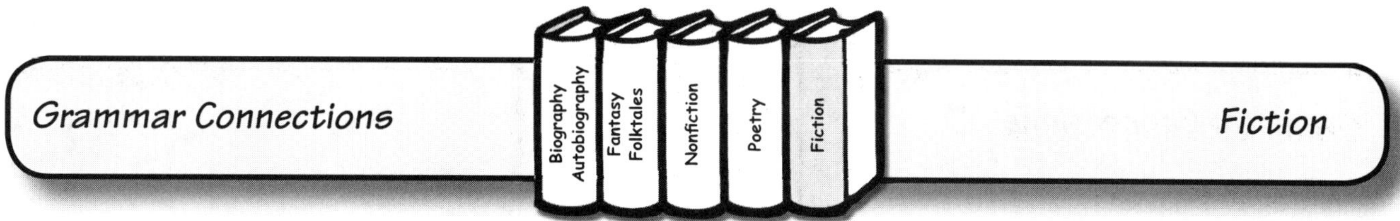

Proofing It All

Errors Page

All fiction writers know a story must be proofread before it can ever be printed. Good writers know to check over their work for any grammar mistakes.

Directions: Read the fiction story below. Look for any capitalization, spelling, or ending punctuation mistakes you can find. When you are finished, correctly rewrite the story on the "Corrections Page" (page 100).

Helpful Hints: There are eight mistakes. All names are spelled correctly.

The Sad Moon

Arawa, the african goddess of the moon, was very happy. Each night she lit up the skye. People on Earth would look up to her and say, "Ah, there is the moon. Isn't she beautyful?"

One night, Arawa grew sad That was a very dark night for Earth, for no moon lit up the sky that night. Adro, the African god of the sky, went to visit Arawa.

"Why are you sad?" Adro asked.

Arawa answered, "i am sad because I am lonely. I am the only lite in the night sky."

"I can help you, Arawa. I will give you friends that will shine with you during the night They will not be as bright as you, but they will keep you company."

So, Adro added stars to the sky. Arawa was happy. The moon lit up the sky once more

---

Proofing It All

Corrections Page

Rewrite the story correctly on this page. Remember, you should have found eight mistakes.

The Sad Moon

Show What You Know

Fiction is a special type of writing. In fiction writing, the author can use his imagination. He can set a story in modern times with modern people, or he can write a story about time traveling. He can create whole new worlds. In nonfiction writing, the author must write about only what is real. He must write about the facts. Both types of writing are interesting to read. In the end, it is up to the reader to decide if he will choose fiction or nonfiction to read from the library shelf.

Directions: Fill in the circle next to the correct answer.

1. Fiction is very different from _________________ .

    (a) fairy tales   **(b)** nonfiction   **(c)** fantasy

2. In fiction writing, the author relies on _________________ .

    (a) imagination   **(b)** facts   **(c)** interviews

3. A fiction story can be set _________________ .

    (a) only in the present   **(b)** only in the past   **(c)** in any time

4. In nonfiction writing, an author can write about _________________ .

    (a) only what is real

    (b) only what is imagined

    (c) both real and imagined things

5. At the library, a person can choose books that _________________ .

    (a) are only fiction

    (b) are only nonfiction

    (c) are interesting to him

Is It True?

Directions: Read each statement. If the statement is true, write **"True"** on the line. If the statement is false, write **"False"** on the line.

_______________ **1.** Fiction is the opposite of nonfiction writing.

_______________ **2.** Fiction is writing that is true or based on facts.

_______________ **3.** A biography would be an example of fiction writing.

_______________ **4.** A story about a fairy living in a magical land would be an example of a fiction story.

_______________ **5.** Fiction is always more interesting than nonfiction.

_______________ **6.** An encyclopedia is a type of fiction book.

_______________ **7.** Nonfiction and fiction are the same type of stories.

_______________ **8.** Historical fiction is based on fact but has some things that are not true.

_______________ **9.** Fairy tales are a type of fiction writing.

_______________ **10.** Dictionaries are fiction.

Reading-Comprehension Test

Story Page

Directions: Read the story below and on page 104.

Sam the Snake

Sam the Snake. That is what everyone called him in the small town of Homestead: Sam the Snake. They called him that for a few reasons. First, he wore a great big, silver belt buckle with a picture of a snake on it. He also wore cowboy boots made out of snakeskin. Plus, when he talked, he sounded a bit like a snake.

"Hey there, boyssssssss," he'd say. "Howsssss it going?"

There were rumors there were even snakes living on his ranch, but no one knew for sure. Sam the Snake was a loner. He was the type of person you wanted to know—but you were afraid to get to know him.

One day, Sam the Snake disappeared. No one knew where he was. The people in the town went to Sheriff Boots to ask what they should do. Sheriff Boots walked across the front porch, the black heels of his boots clicking on the wood. He hiked up his pants, cleared his throat, and slowly spoke.

"Well, Sam the Snake is a grown man. He can come and go as he pleases. Unless you have proof that something is wrong, I can't help you."

There was a little boy in town that no one paid much attention to, except when he got into trouble. His name was Tommy. He was about eight or nine years old. His mother worked several jobs. She did her best to take care of Tommy, but she was so busy and so tired that she did not have the energy to raise him properly.

Tommy liked Sam the Snake. He liked the way he slithered into the town. He liked the respect people showed him. He liked the way Sam showed respect to other people, as well. He would hold doors open for people, tip his hat, say "please" and "thank you," and help people who needed help if he saw the need.

Tommy was upset that Sam the Snake was missing. He felt that something was wrong. Tommy knew he was only a boy, but he believed that he had to do whatever he could to find out if Sam was in trouble.

He decided to check out Sam the Snake's ranch first. He was a little scared to enter the house. He, too, had heard the rumors of the snakes. But he felt it was the right thing to do.

Reading-Comprehension Test

Story Page *(cont.)*

Sam the Snake *(cont.)*

He entered through a small window. There were no live snakes that he could see. What he did find was that everything was in its place. In fact, it looked like Sam had planned to be gone for a while.

Then Tommy noticed that Sam's snakeskin boots were there. And his belt buckle was there, too.

Tommy panicked. He started to run. He ran toward the big city that was far away. Maybe the sheriff of the big city would help him. After awhile, he began to wish he had his bike and some water. Soon, his legs gave out. He fell to the ground, exhausted and crying.

"What'sssss wrong, Thomassssssss?" he heard.

Tommy gasped. "You know my name?"

"Of coursssssssse," said Sam the Snake. "Where are you going?"

"I was looking for you!"

"Me? Why? No one ever looksss for me."

"I was worried about you. We were all worried about you. Where were you?"

"I was lonely," said Sam the Snake. "I went to the big cccity to sssee if I could meet sssomeone ssspecial. But the big cccity is too big for me. I like it better back in Homessstead, even if I am lonely."

"Lonely?" questioned Tommy. "You? Do you know how many people would like to be your friend in our town? There are tons!" Tommy paused a moment then asked, "Hey Sam, why did you leave your boots at home and your buckle?"

"I thought those old bootsss might ssscare away the ladiesss," Sam told him.

That night, and on many nights to come, Sam the Snake ate dinner with Tommy and his mother. Soon, Tommy's mother started wearing dresses in snakeskin prints, and Tommy started wearing snakeskin boots that were just his size.

And that is how a small boy who no one paid attention to changed the lives of many people. And that is how the town learned that everyone, even a person like Sam the Snake, needs a friend.

Reading-Comprehension Test

Questions Page

Directions: Answer each question about the story you read.

1. In what city did Sam the Snake live? _______________________________________

2. When Sam talked, what was unusual about his speech or the way he spoke?

   ____

3. People thought Sam the Snake might have what animals living on his ranch?

   ____

4. What unusual thing happened one day with Sam the Snake?

   ____

5. Why did the sheriff believe the people should not be worried about Sam the Snake?

   ____

   ____

6. What did Tommy find when he went to Sam the Snake's house?

   ____

7. Why did finding these things upset Tommy? ___________________________________

   ____

8. Where had Sam the Snake been all along?______________________________________

9. Why did he go there? ____

   ____

10. At the end of the story, do you think Sam was still lonely? How do you know?

   ____

   ____

Something Extra: On the back of this page, draw a picture of Tommy with Sam the Snake. Be sure to color your picture when you are finished.

More with Sam

Directions: Use the story "Sam the Snake" (pages 103–104) to help you complete the assignment below.

1. "Sam the Snake" is a fiction story. What makes this story a fiction story?

2. Who are the main characters in "Sam the Snake"?

3. Every fiction story has a plot. What is the plot of "Sam the Snake"?

4. Most fiction stories have a theme or a lesson the reader can learn from the story. The theme of "Sam the Snake" is given in the last paragraph. Write the theme:

What Have You Learned?

Directions: Read and answer each one.

1. Define the word *fiction*. ____

   ____

2. How is fiction different from nonfiction? _______________________________

   ____

3. Show you recognize fiction by listing some titles. Use books from the library, your home, or the classroom and write the titles of three fiction books. Also, list each author's name.

   Book #1

   Title: ____

   Author: ____

   Book #2

   Title: ____

   Author: ____

   Book #3

   Title: ____

   Author: ____

4. Look at the books you used to complete question #3. Write the name of those three authors in alphabetical order. Use the authors' last names to place them in order. For example, "Jane Smith" would be "Smith, Jane."

   1. ____

   2. ____

   3. ____

5. Give an example of a book that would *not* be a fiction book.

   ____

Classify It

Event Strips

Fiction is writing that has events that are pretend or not true. Much of what happens in a fiction book is from the author's imagination. The fiction author can include some real people, places, or events, but he does not write a story about real or true things. Nonfiction writing is the opposite of fiction. Nonfiction writing is filled with events that are true or that have happened. Nonfiction books are based on facts where fiction books are not.

Directions: Cut out each event listed below. Decide whether each event would be fiction or nonfiction. Tape or glue each event strip under the correct heading on the "Which Is It?" sheet (page 109).

Events

The moon comes out at night.

The man in the moon winked at me.

The horse and chariot helped the sun move across the sky.

The sun warmed up the Earth.

My sister is a pest.

My sister's fairy godmother turned her into a princess.

The video game was fun.

The characters came out of the video game and played with my toys.

My stomach yelled, "I'm hungry!"

My stomach growled because I was hungry.

The farmer fed his three horses.

The farmer fed his three unicorns.

Classify It

Which Is It?

Fiction

1.
2.
3.
4.
5.
6.

Nonfiction

1.
2.
3.
4.
5.
6.

Just For Fun: Choose one of the events you listed in the fiction section. Write a short fiction story and use the event in your story.

Gopher It!

Directions: Color only the gophers that have information that is true about fiction writing.

Choose Your Answer

Fiction writing is writing where the author uses his imagination. He can create characters, places, and events. He can create entire worlds. Much of what appears in a fiction book is pretend. However, the author can use some real people or events in a fiction book if he chooses to do so. Fiction writing that uses real people or events from the past is called historical fiction. In nonfiction, however, the author must write *only* what is true or based on facts. Both types of writing are fun to read. It is up to the reader to decide which type of book he will choose!

Directions: Choose the correct answer by filling in the circle.

1. Fiction is writing where the author uses _______________________.

   (a) only facts

   (b) his imagination

2. A fiction author can create _______________________.

   (a) only what is true or real

   (b) entire new worlds

3. Much of what appears in fiction books is _______________________.

   (a) based on real events

   (b) from the author's imagination

4. Fiction writing that has some real characters or events is called _______________________.

   (a) historical fiction

   (b) science fiction

5. The opposite of fiction writing is _______________________.

   (a) nonfiction writing

   (b) letter writing

6. In nonfiction writing, the author can use only information that is _______________________.

   (a) pretend

   (b) true

Understanding the Story

Story Page

Directions: Read the following fiction story. Then answer the questions on page 113.

On the Beach

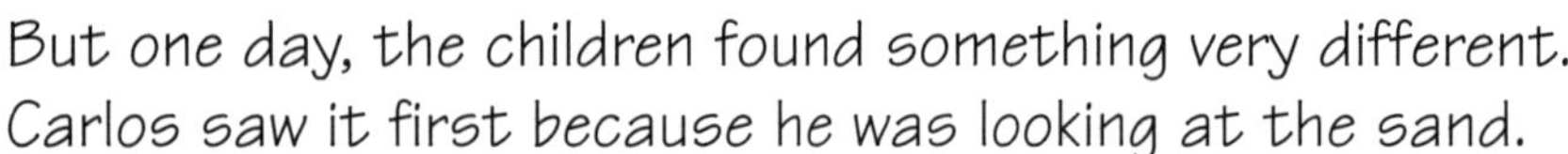

Carlos and Mary often went to the beach. Carlos liked to pick up shells, and Mary enjoyed watching the birds.

But one day, the children found something very different. Carlos saw it first because he was looking at the sand.

"Mary," said Carlos, "Come here quickly. You won't believe this!"

Mary stopped watching the seagulls dive and swoop. She ran over to where Carlos was standing. She saw he was looking down at a long, brown-gray, fishy kind of animal.

"What is it?" asked Mary.

"I think it's a small shark," answered Carlos.

Mary looked at the sharp teeth and pointy fins. "I think you're right, Carlos," she agreed.

"Is it still alive?" Carlos asked Mary.

"No," Mary answered sadly. "Sharks can't live out of water."

The children looked at the shark a long time. Finally Carlos said, "It is time to go home. But I can't wait to tell Mom about what we found on the beach!"

Understanding the Story

Questions Page

Directions: Use "On the Beach" (page 112) to answer the following questions.

1. What did Carlos like to do when he went to the beach? _______________________

   ____

2. Who first saw the unusual creature on the beach? _________________________

   ____

3. What did Mary enjoy doing while at the beach? ___________________________

   ____

4. What did Carlos find on the beach? _____________________________________

   ____

5. Why do you think the shark was no longer alive? _________________________

   ____

6. Why do you think Carlos wanted to tell his mother about what he'd found?

   ____

   ____

7. Have you ever been to the beach? __________ If yes, did you enjoy your time at the beach? If no, do you think you would ever like to go to the beach?

   ____

   ____

8. What would be another good title for this story?

   ____

Fiction or Nonfiction?

Directions: Read the following story. Then answer the questions that follow.

Snakes

Have you ever held a snake? Did you think it would feel slimy?

Snakes are not slimy. If they are healthy, they are dry and smooth. Their bodies are covered with scales. Even their eyes are covered with see-through scales instead of eyelids.

Snakes can swim through water, climb up trees, crawl along ropes, and slither across the ground. The Black Mamba snake is one of the fastest snakes. It can travel up to 12 miles an hour.

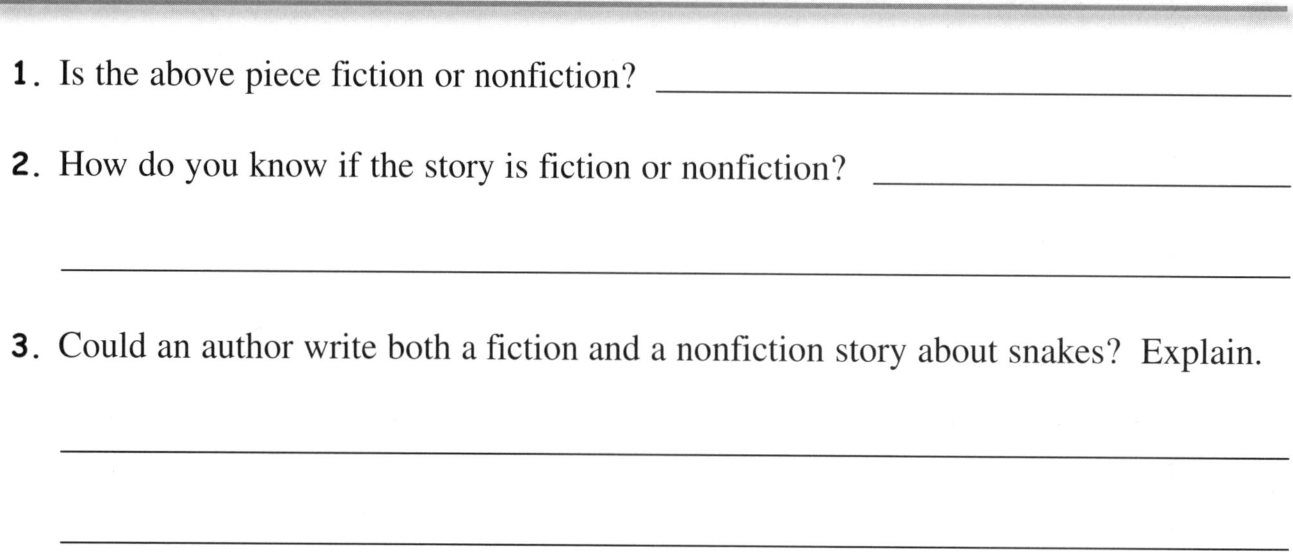

Snakes are cold-blooded, and most snakes sleep through the winter. All snakes swallow their food whole and shed their skin when it gets too tight.

Snakes don't hear, but they feel sounds with their bodies. Snakes taste and smell with their tongues.

1. Is the above piece fiction or nonfiction? _______________________

2. How do you know if the story is fiction or nonfiction? _______________________

   ____

3. Could an author write both a fiction and a nonfiction story about snakes? Explain.

   ____

   ____

Fiction or Nonfiction?

Your Own Snake Story

Directions: Show you understand fiction. Use the space below to write a fiction story about snakes.

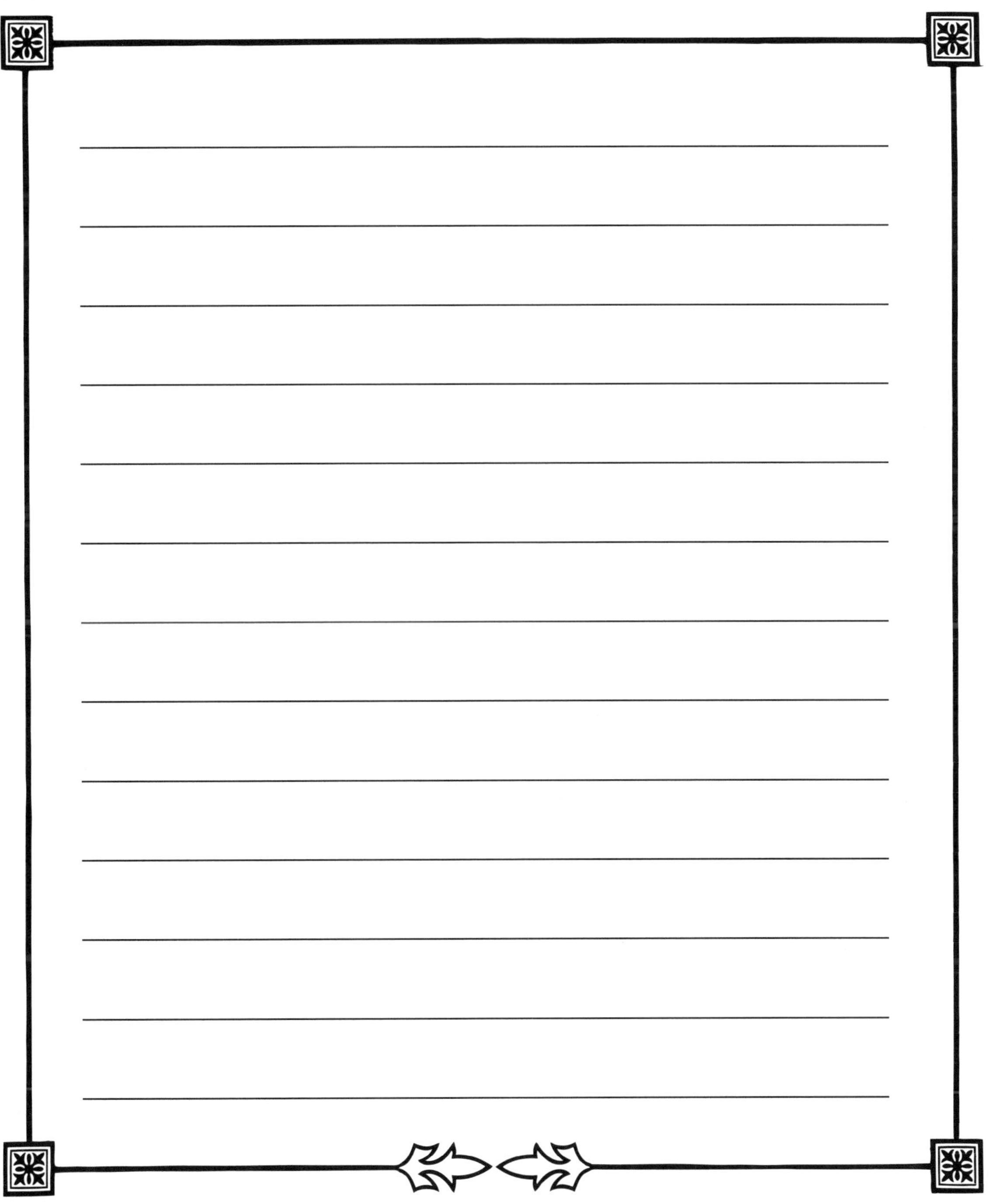

Seeing Is Believing

Directions: Try your hand at drawing your answers instead of writing your answers. Follow the directions in each section to show you understand what fiction is all about.

1. Draw and color a picture of a character that could only appear in a fantasy fiction book.

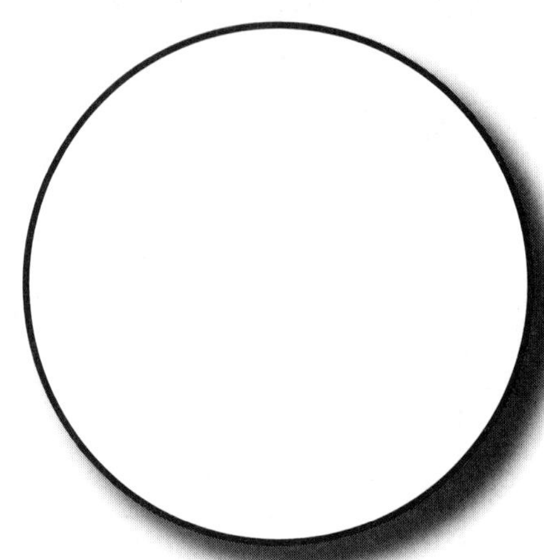

2. Draw and color a book cover for a fiction book about a young girl who goes into her closet to get her school clothes but suddenly enters into a magical world made of candy.

3. Pretend you are a character in a historical fiction book. Now draw and color a picture of yourself at some famous historical event. For example, you might have been present when the Wright brothers made their famous flight, or maybe you were there when Neil Armstrong walked on the moon!

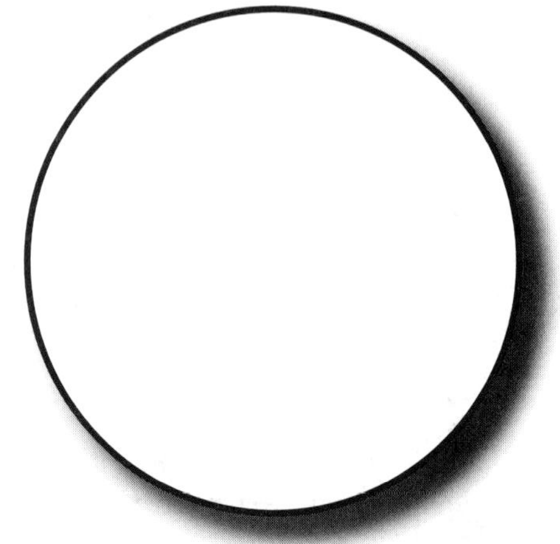

Finding the Answer

Directions: Use the words in the box to help you fill in the blanks in the story below.

library	fiction	pretend
imagination	nonfiction	historical

Fiction writing is writing that has characters, settings, or events that are

(1) ________________________. Fiction writing is created from the author's

(2) ________________________.

Fiction writing that is based on real events of the past but that has some

elements that are from the author's imagination is called (3) ________________

fiction. There are actually many types of (4) ________________________ stories.

Fantasy and fairy tales are examples of fiction writing. (5) ________________________

writing is different than fiction in that it must be based on facts or what is true.

Fiction writing can all be based on the author's imagination. If you want to read

some enjoyable fiction or nonfiction books, you should go to the

(6) ________________________ and check out some great books!

Show You Know

Materials:

- notebook paper
- scissors
- two boxes
- chalk or markers and board
- list of students' names cut into strips
- timer or clock

Directions: Think of the titles of five fiction stories you know. You can use fairy tales, short stories, stories read to you by the teacher, or any other fiction titles you know. Write the fiction titles on a piece of paper. Write your name underneath each title. Cut the titles into five strips. Give the paper strips to your teacher. The teacher will place the strips into one box. In a separate box, the teacher will have the names of each student in the class.

When everyone is finished writing their titles, the teacher will draw one title from the box. The student whose name is written under the title will come up and help the teacher watch the timer. The teacher will also draw one student name from the second box. The second student whose name is drawn will come up and silently read the title the teacher is holding. The student will then try to draw clues on the board so the students in the class can guess what book title is on the piece of paper. The student will only have two minutes to draw. The student watching the timer is not allowed to make a guess.

The student doing the drawing cannot talk. However, if someone in the class guesses part of the title correctly, he or she can write the correctly-guessed words on the board. The student who raises his or her hand and answers the entire title correctly will then be chosen by the teacher to be the next person to draw on the board.

All students should keep a list of the titles that are drawn from the box. When students are finished with the game, the teacher will place students back into their groups. Students will then look at their lists and circle five books on each list. The students must find out the authors of the five books they have circled.

Students can keep these lists with them at all times to have a handy reference for a list of great fiction books.

Light Bright

Directions: Color only the light bulbs that are bright enough to have information that is true about fiction written next to them. Put an **X** over the other bulbs.

 **1.** Fiction is based on facts.

 **6.** Biographies are a type of fiction.

 **2.** Fiction writing must always be true.

 **7.** There are many types of fiction stories.

 **3.** A fiction author can use his imagination.

 **8.** An encyclopedia is an example of a fiction book.

 **4.** Fiction is the opposite of nonfiction.

 **9.** A dictionary is not a fiction book.

 **5.** Fairy tales are a type of fiction.

 **10.** Fantasy books are a type of fiction.

Check for Understanding

Story Page

Directions: Read the fiction story. Answer the questions that follow on page 121.

A Long Way to Travel

Kristen and her mother were walking on the beach. There had been a terrible storm the day before, and a lot of interesting things had washed up on the beach that day.

"Look at this, Mom," Kristen said to her mother. She pointed excitedly at a piece of round, blue glass. The glass was almost completely covered with sand. It was amazing that Kristen had even been able to see it. Kristen and her mother dug around the blue glass. They were surprised to find a beautiful, round, glass ball. When Kristen held it in her hands, she saw that it was bigger than a softball but smaller than a soccer ball.

"What is it?" Kristen asked her mother.

"It's a fisherman's float," her mother explained. "I haven't seen one of these in years. The storm must have washed it onto the beach."

"What's a fisherman's float?" Kristen asked.

"Japanese fishermen once used these to keep their nets from sinking," Kristen's mother explained.

"Then that means this came all the way from Japan!" Kristen exclaimed. "Wow! It's traveled more than I have!"

"Maybe someday you can go to Japan," Kristen's mother said.

"Maybe I will," Kristen agreed. "Maybe I will."

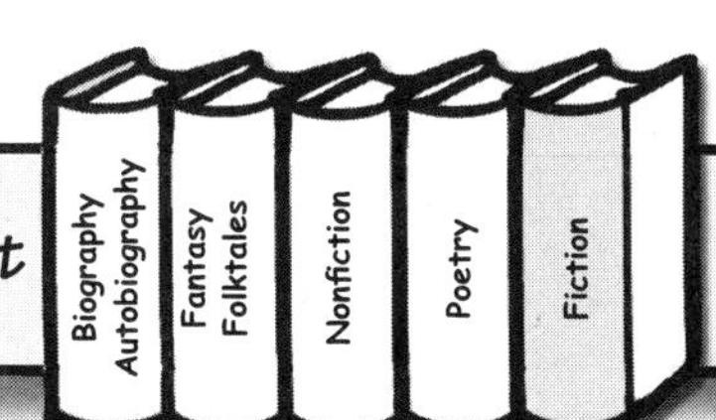

Check for Understanding

Questions Page

Directions: Fill in the circle next to the correct answer.

1. Why did Kristen and her mom go for a walk on the beach?

(a) to see what the storm had brought up on the beach

(b) to check a sea turtle's nest

2. What special thing did Kristen find in the sand?

(a) a hermit crab   (b) a blue ball

3. The ball Kristen found was __________________.

(a) smaller than a baseball   (b) smaller than a basketball

4. Kristen's mother explained that the blue ball was ________________.

(a) a fisherman's float   (b) a fisherman's crystal ball

5. Why was Kristen's mother surprised to see the float?

(a) because it was worth a lot of money

(b) because she had not seen one in years

6. Kristen was amazed to think the float had come from ______________.

(a) Japan   (b) the ocean

7. Kristen's mother thought the float might make Kristen want to ________________.

(a) travel to Japan   (b) become a ship's captain

8. Another good title for this story might be __________________.

(a) "The Special Surprise"   (b) "The Short Journey"

The Perfect School

Describe with Words

In fiction writing, an author can create anything he wants. Imagine you can use fiction-writing skills to create a perfect school.

Directions: In the space below, describe what a perfect school would be like. You can describe as many parts of the school as you want, but be sure to include the following in your description:

- ✎ *the classroom*
- ✎ *the playground*

- ✎ *the teachers*
- ✎ *the cafeteria*

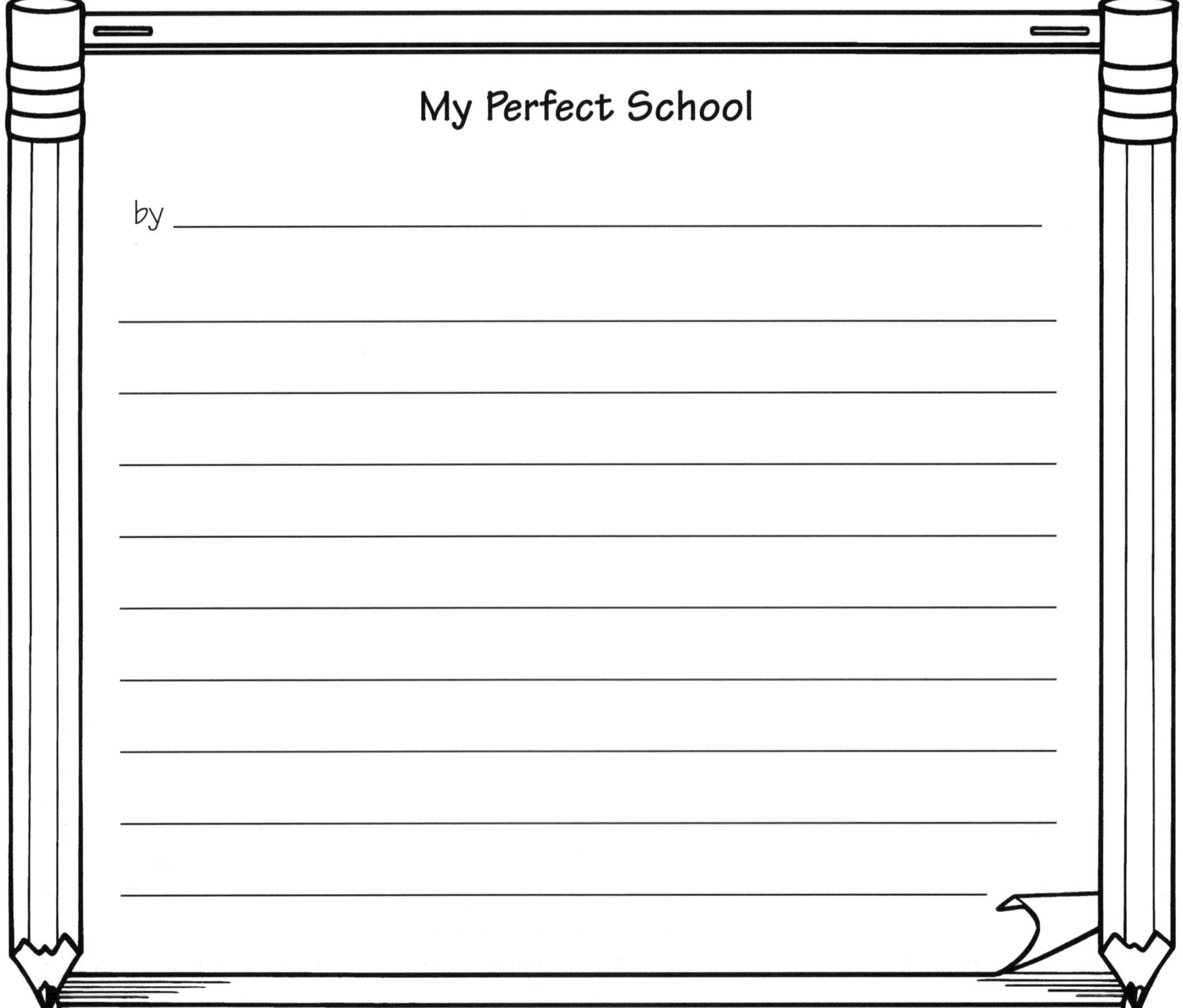

The Perfect School

Describe with Images

Directions: Use your written description from the first part of this exercise ("Describe with Words," page 122) to help you put your art skills to work.

In the space below, use what you have written to help you draw your perfect classroom.

The Perfect Student

One job of a fiction author is to create fiction characters.

Use what you already know about school and create a perfect student for a fiction book. Remember, in a fiction book, anything is possible for your perfect student!

Directions: Complete each blank to help you create the perfect student.

1. Student's name: ____

2. Student's grade: ____

3. Student's hair color and eye color: ____________________________

4. Name of student's school: _____________________________________

5. This student's last report card grades looked like this: ➡

6. This student is really great at the following:

____

____

7. This student made the school better when he/she __________________

____

____

8. The principal really likes this student because ___________________

____

____

Just For Fun: On the back of this page, draw and color a picture of your perfect student.

Try Your Hand

One really fun thing about fiction is that anything is possible. A fiction story is all about imagination. Look at the activity below and try your hand at using your imagination.

Directions: In the middle of the hand below, write your name. Then use your imagination to complete the rest of the hand. On each finger, write something fantastic you wish you could do but can't. Use your imagination. Remember, anything is possible in fiction.

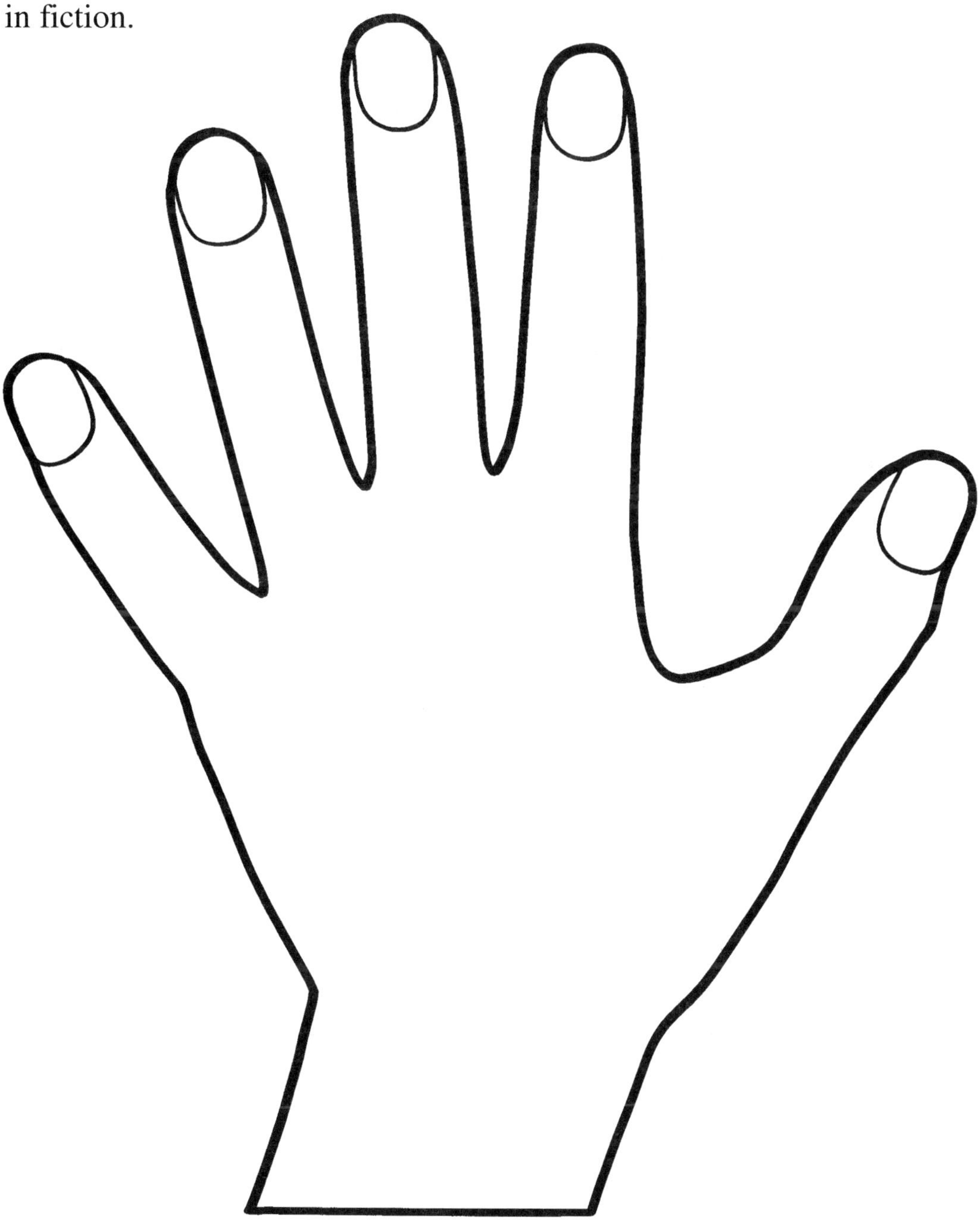

Your Reading Quilt

Instructions Page

Quilts are beautiful blankets that are handmade from different pieces of material. Sometimes a person making a quilt will use pieces of material from items that have a special meaning. One quilt piece may be from a favorite shirt or an outfit worn on a special occasion. When the quilt is finished, the person has a quilt filled with memories of special events. Sometimes a person will make a quilt as a gift. The quilter will share her special skills with some other lucky person. Use what you know about quilts to help you complete the reading quilt on the following page.

Directions for Making a Reading Quilt

✎ Think of your favorite fiction books. Write down several titles and the authors of these books.

✎ Once you have written down several titles, narrow your list down to five choices. Make sure you are willing to share these book titles with your class.

✎ Use the "Quilt Pattern" sheet (page 127) to help you share your favorite fiction books with your class. In each square that does not already have a design, write the title of a favorite fiction book. Also, write the author's name and draw a small picture to illustrate the book.

✎ Color the quilt when you are finished so that your teacher can hang it on the classroom wall and share your favorites with the rest of the class.

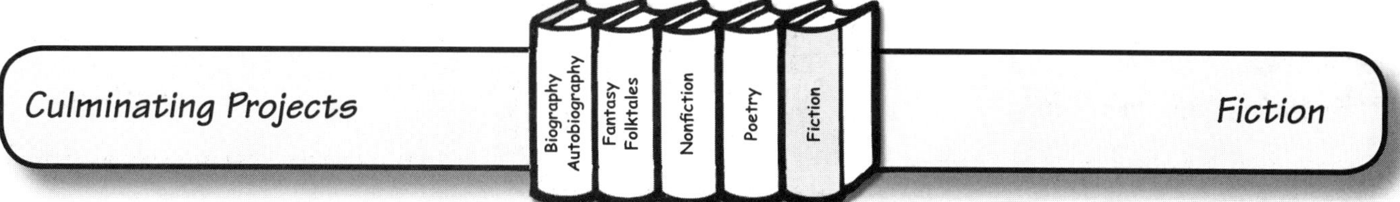

Your Reading Quilt

Quilt Pattern

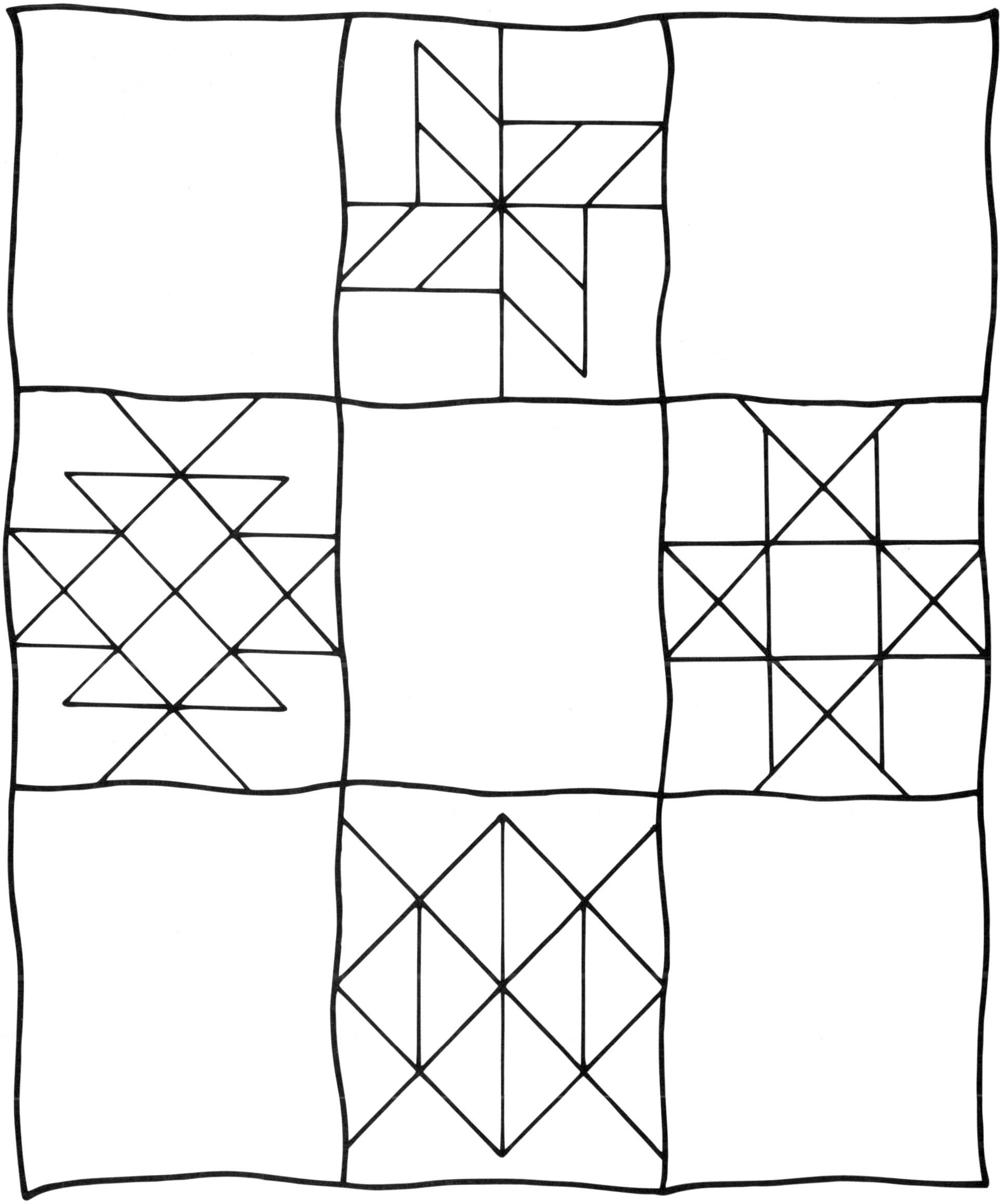

Putting a Fiction Story to Music

Most everyone has a favorite fiction story. Sometimes the book is one you read by yourself. Or maybe your teacher read a fiction book to the class and you loved it. It does not matter where the book came from, as long as it is a book you really liked.

Think of a fiction story you have enjoyed and use that story to help you complete the following activity.

Directions: Think of a familiar tune. Use the tune to help you create a new song about a favorite fiction book. Make sure the song you write gives information about your favorite book.

Helpful Hint: Can't think of a tune? Try "Twinkle, Twinkle Little Star" or "B-I-N-G-O."

Fiction book title: ____

Sung to this tune: ____

____

____

____

____

____

____

____

____

Television and Fiction

Much of what is on television is fiction. Fiction is anything that is not true or is pretend. Since many television shows have to be written as a script before they are performed, such shows have a lot in common with fiction books. Just like a book, most television shows must have characters, settings, and plots.

Directions: Use a favorite television program (or movie) to help answer these questions.

1. What is the name of the television show you like to watch?

2. What are some clues that help you know this is a fiction show?

3. Who are the main characters of your favorite show?

4. Where is the setting of the show?

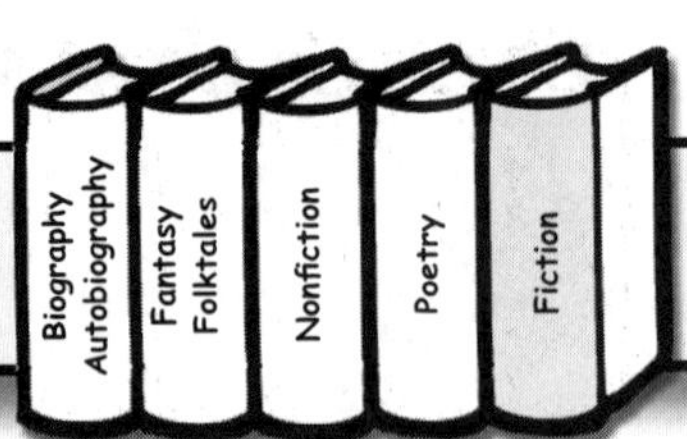

Library Detective

Directions: Go to your school's library or the public library and use the information you find to help you answer each question.

1. What is the name of your school's librarian?

____

2. Which section of your school's library is larger, the fiction or the nonfiction section?

____

3. What is the very first fiction title and author's name listed in the "A" section of the fiction section?

____

4. From which section of the library are you most likely to check out a book?

____

5. Find a fiction book with a title that starts with the same letter as your first name. Write down the title of the book and the author's name.

____

6. Before you leave the library, check out a fiction book. Write down the title and the name of the author:

____

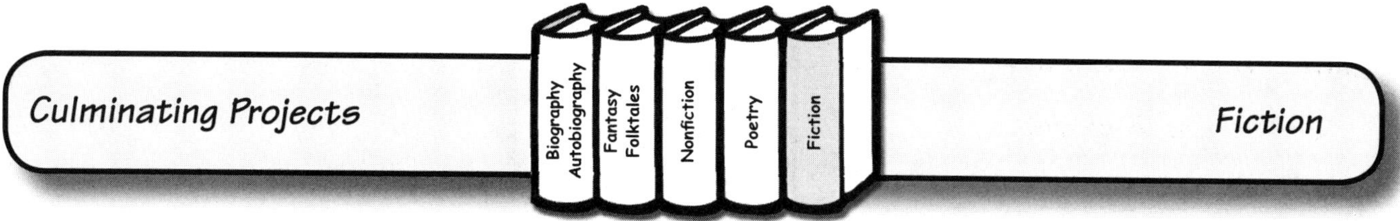

Using a Story Starter

Directions: Use the following story starter to help you write your own fiction story.

The puppy was scared. He was alone. He had been left in a cardboard box outside of a store, and it was starting to rain. Where had the pretty, young girl gone? Where had his brothers and sisters gone? He didn't know what to do, but somehow he knew he couldn't just stay in the box forever. He was hungry and cold. It was time to do something.

____

____

____

____

____

____

____

____

____

____

Choose and Start

Part I

Directions: Look at the columns below. Choose as many items as you want from each column. Use the ones you choose in a story you create. Write your story on the page that follows. (You can add in new character names of your own, but you must use some given on the list, too.)

Titles

"The Crazy Day"

"My Mother, the Giraffe"

"The Mystery Gift"

"All Good Things"

"The Secret"

"The Hidden Treasure"

"Something Special"

"Above the Clouds"

"Camping in the Park"

Settings

the Wild West

New York City

the beach

Shalah, a magical land

the mall

a dark and scary forest

the zoo

the desert

a magical castle

a fluffy, white cloud

Characters

Leonard Lion

Suzy Shamrock

Randolph Rabbit

twins Sandy and Mandy

Tommy Zookeeper

Sally Snake

Kara, a small fairy

Princess Gina

King Carl

Samson

Opening Lines

Once upon a time . . .

I couldn't believe it . . .

We were so surprised . . .

It was time to get up . . .

Have you ever had one of those days . . .

No one knew how long it had been there . . .

It was a dark and stormy night . . .

On the day of her birthday . . .

They knew something was wrong . . .

Where did they go?

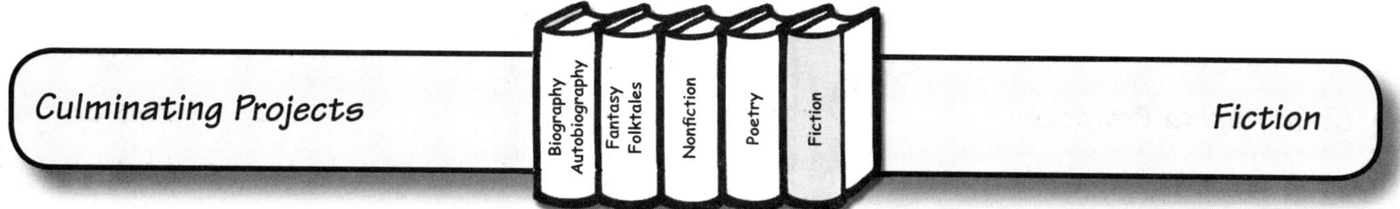

Choose and Start

Part II

Directions: Use the story parts from your Part I worksheet (page 132) to write a story.

Story Title: _______________________________

Your Name: _______________________________

____

____

____

____

____

____

____

____

____

____

____

____

Summarize and Sequence

A Visual Book Report

Choose a fiction book for this project. Read it and complete the activity below.

Directions: You are to complete a book report about a fiction book. Use the squares below to help you summarize and put into sequential order the events of your book.

Use the boxes to draw pictures, like a cartoon strip, of the events that occur in the fiction book you read. Start with the first events of the book and go through until the end. You must decide which events are most important because you cannot add boxes.

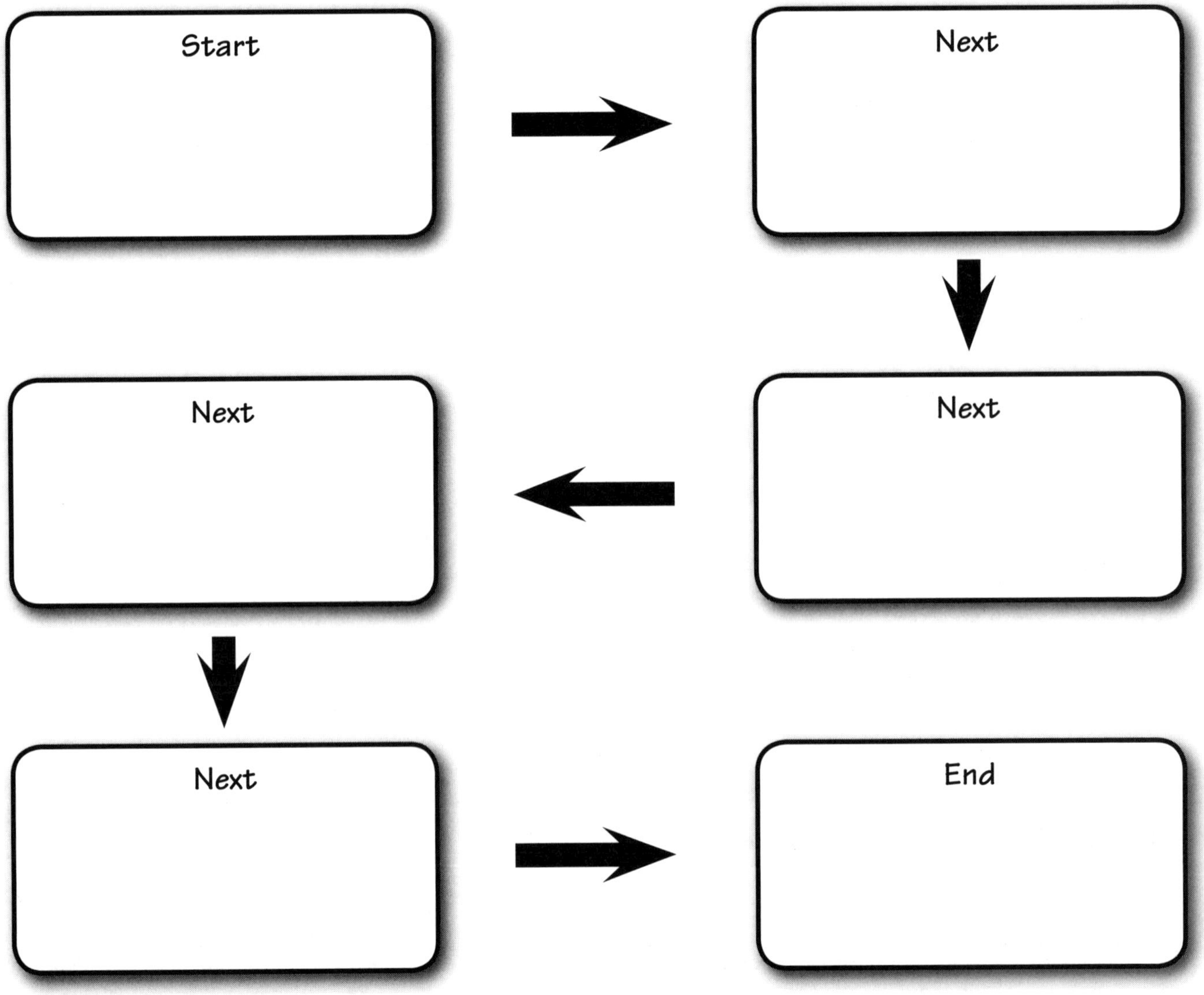

Start	**Next**
Next	**Next**
Next	**End**

Telling About Fiction

Directions: After you have finished reading a fiction book, answer the following questions. Be prepared to use the questions to help you tell the class about the book you read.

1. Book title: ____

2. Author's name: ____

3. Have you read any other books by this author? __________ If yes, what were they?

   ____

   ____

4. Who were the main characters? ________________________________

   ____

5. Briefly tell about the book: __________________________________

   ____

6. Did you like the book? Why or why not? ________________________

   ____

7. Would you recommend this book to a friend? ____________________

8. Explain your answer to question #7. ___________________________

   ____

Popular Fiction

Many fiction books today are very popular throughout the world. A book and its characters may become so popular that they are often used on such everyday products such as to-go meals, toys, and cereal boxes.

Directions: Choose a fiction book. Decorate the front of the cereal box using the title and important information from your book. Be sure to color the box when you are finished.

Make a Plate Person

Materials:

- white paper plate
- yarn
- markers, crayons, or coloring pencils
- glue

Directions: Draw the face of your favorite fiction character on the white paper plate. Use yarn as needed for hair, fur, etc. Write the name of your character on the back of the plate.

Complete the following questions. Do not tell your classmates who your character is. When called on by your teacher, you will use the questions below to give clues to the class about who your character is. The first student to correctly guess the character will then get to tell about his or her book character.

1. Some words that would describe my character are ______________________________

____

2. My character is friends/enemies with ___________________________________

3. My character lives at ____

4. One special thing about my character is _________________________________

____

5. The name of the book my character is in is _______________________________

____

Character Display

Materials:

- a shoebox
- markers, crayons, or coloring pencils
- glue
- construction paper
- index card

Directions: Read a fiction story where one of the characters is not a person. Then follow these directions:

✎ Use your shoebox to create a home for your character. Design a home inside the shoebox. (You will not need the box's lid.) The shoebox design should be drawn on the inside of the box on the largest section. You can use any materials you want to design your character's habitat. Be sure to include your character, too! Remember to use information from the book to help make your creation.

✎ When you are finished with your shoebox habitat, write a short paragraph on your index card. The paragraph should describe your character and his/her/its habitat. Be sure to write the name of the book you read at the top of the index card. Put your name on the back of the index card.

✎ Place your box where your teacher directs you. Place the index card in front of the box.

✎ When all the boxes are complete, you and your classmates will enjoy walking by, viewing, and reading about some wonderful fiction characters. If you are lucky, you might even find a new book to read!

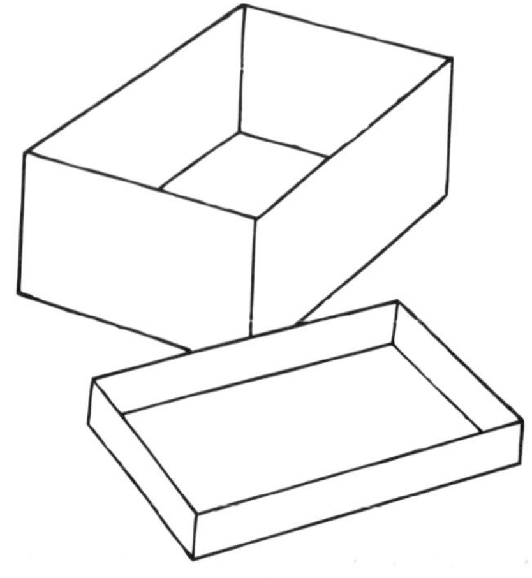

Art-Tastic!

So many wonderful fiction books are being made into movies. Use your skills as an artist to help promote your favorite book.

Directions: Pretend your favorite fiction book is about to be turned into a movie. You have been asked to design the movie poster. Use the space below to draw and color your poster.

Note: If your favorite book has already been made into a movie, then design a poster that is different from the one that was already created for it.

A Valentine for a Character

Instructions Page

Materials:

- construction or craft paper
- glue
- crayons or markers
- heart pattern (page 141)
- staples and stapler

Directions: Use the heart on the next piece of paper to help design a valentine card to a favorite fictional book character.

✎ Cut out the heart. Place the heart on a piece of construction or craft paper. Use the heart as a stencil by tracing around the heart. Cut out the new heart on the colored piece of paper. This new piece will be the top of your card. The original, white heart will be the back of your card.

✎ Place the construction-paper heart on top of the original heart. Staple the hearts at the top so that the card opens from the bottom point.

✎ Add any decorations you would like to the front of your card.

✎ Open to the inside of your card. Fill in the "To" and "From" section of the card. The "To" section should be to your favorite fictional character from a book. The "From" section should be from you.

✎ Write a short sentiment or message to your character. Be sure to tell the character why he/she/it is your favorite!

A Valentine for a Character

Pattern Page

Directions: Cut out the heart below. Use the heart to help create your book character valentine.

To: From:

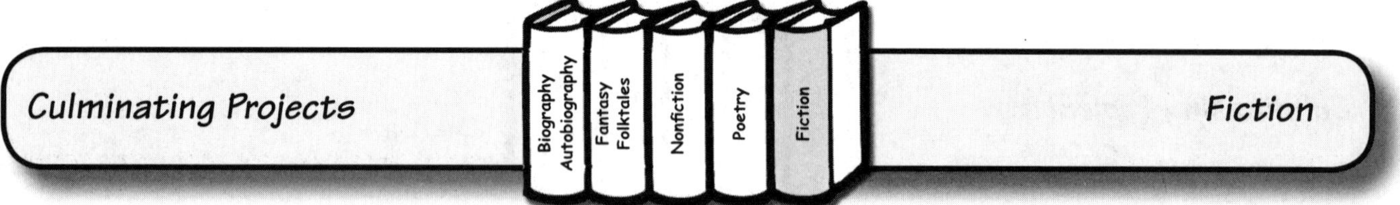

Write to Your Favorite Character

Directions: Use the space below to write a letter to your favorite book character. Be sure to ask your character plenty of questions and give your opinion on things that happened in the book.

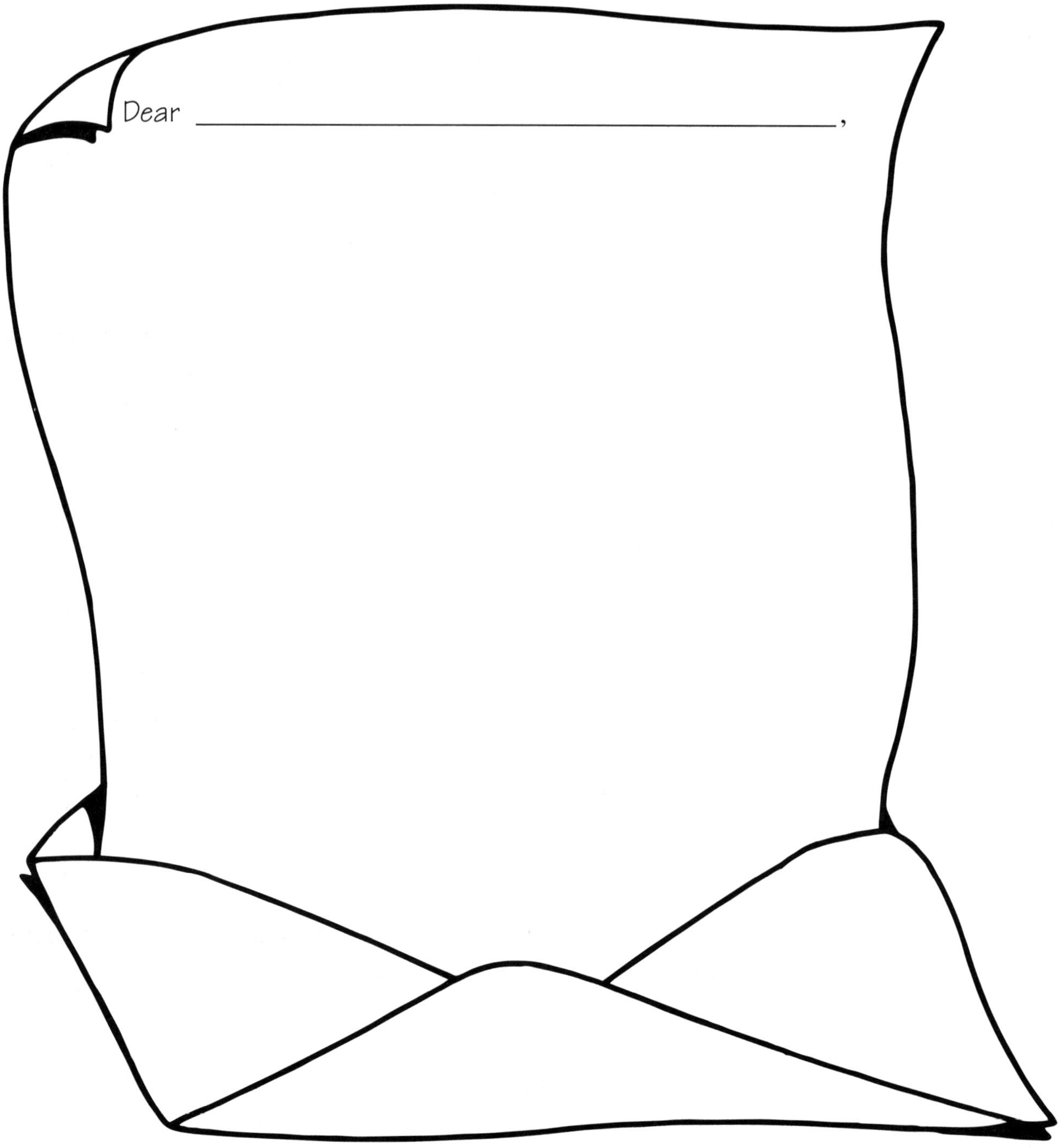

Dear ________________________________,

Cut-Out Character

Material:

- glue
- magazines
- paper
- scissors
- pencil

Directions: Choose a favorite fictional book character. Think about the character and what he/she/it looks like.

- Take a piece of white paper and write the name of your character at the top. Be sure to include the title of the book where you first "met" the character.

- Now comes the fun part! Go through magazines and try and find images that remind you of your character. Piece together pictures that help you recreate the character. For example, your character may have had blue eyes. Find a pair of blue eyes and add them to your page. Maybe your character always ate chocolate. Find some chocolate and add to your page. You may actually find enough pictures to make a collage of your character, or you may only find pictures that remind you of your character. Either way is correct.

- Be sure to include lots of pictures. Leave very little white showing on your page.

Helpful Hint: To help your collage of pictures look nice and neat, learn to use your glue sparingly. It does not take a lot of glue to affix or hold a magazine picture. Try to put the glue only around the edges of what you have cut out. This will stop you from having lumps and bumps underneath the most important part of the picture!

Book-Fair Fun

Materials:

- poster board
- pencil
- markers or crayons
- construction paper, glue, or other craft materials (*optional*)

Directions: Many schools have book fairs that come to their libraries. When a book fair comes to a school, the library is often decorated with posters advertising the exciting new books that will be for sale.

✎ Pretend your class is about to have its own book fair. The books you are advertising aren't for sale, but they can be checked out.

✎ Go to your school's library and check out a fiction book. Read the book and make sure it is a book that you really like.

✎ Now design a poster to advertise your book to other students in the school. Use the poster to convince students to check out the book.

✎ Be sure to give enough information to make the book interesting, but remember not to tell anything about the book that would spoil it for the next reader!

✎ Make sure the poster includes the title of the book and the author's name so anyone who reads your poster can easily find the book on the library's shelves.

Learning Vocabulary

Directions: As you read, you may come across a word that is new to you. Write the word in the center of the graph. Follow the directions given to complete the graph.

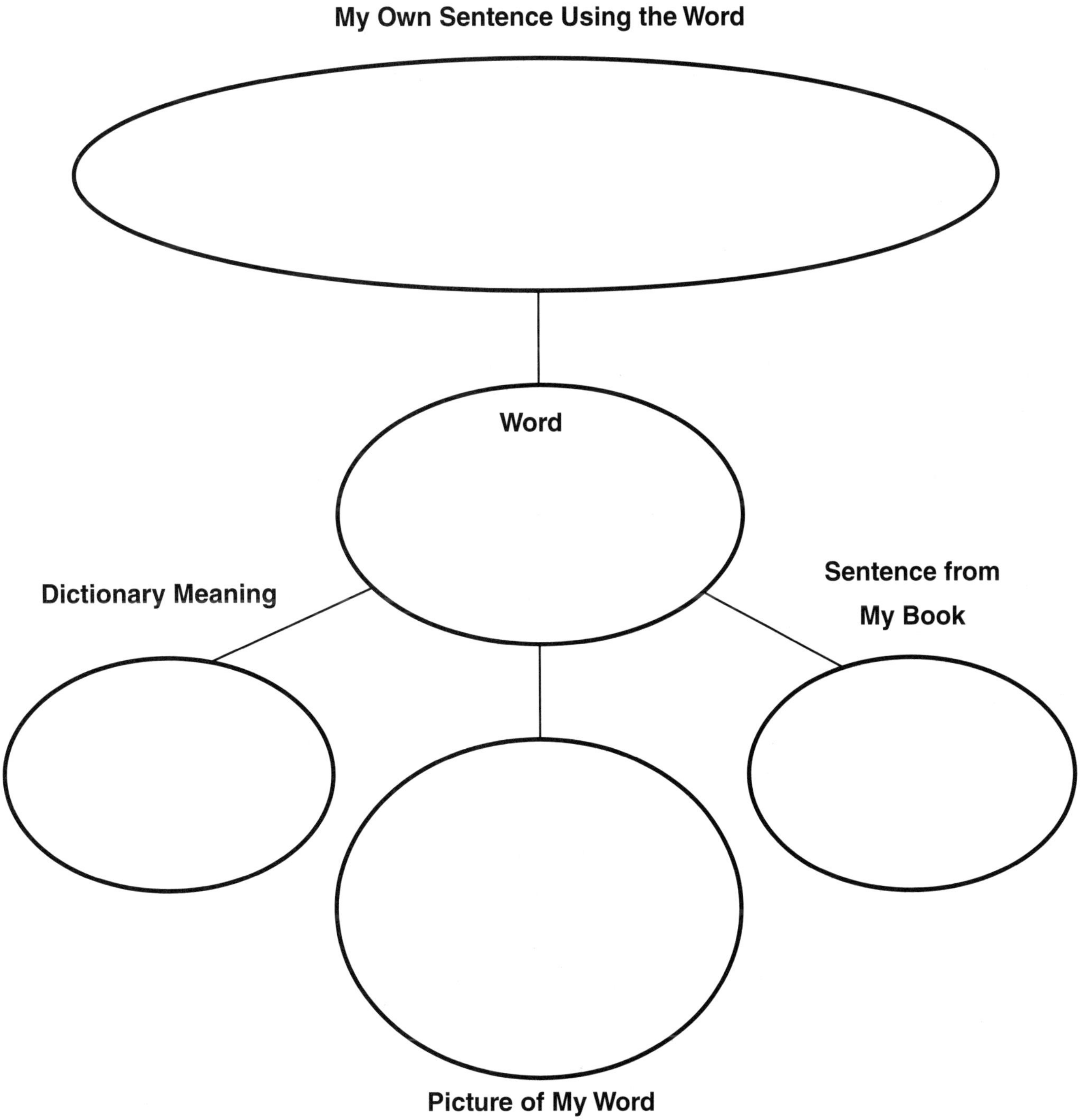

My Own Sentence Using the Word

Word

Dictionary Meaning

Sentence from My Book

Picture of My Word

More with Vocabulary

Directions: As you read your book, look for words that are unfamiliar to you. Complete the blank graph below using the new words you have found. Two examples have been done to show you how to use the graph.

New Word	What is it?
aphid	The bug is eating mom's roses.
barbells	The things my dad has under the bed.

New Word	What is it?

I Know What That Means!

Directions:

1. As you read, find a word that is new to you.

2. Write what you think it means on the "My guess" line.

3. Now look up the word in the dictionary. If your guess was right, check the box. If not, write what the word means on the line.

4. Find another word and do the same.

Word: ___________________________

My guess: _________________________

____

____

I guessed right! ❏

Now I know it means ______________

____

____

____

____

____

Word: ___________________________

My guess: _________________________

____

____

I guessed right! ❏

Now I know it means ______________

____

____

____

____

____

Favorite Book Words

Directions: As you read, find words that fit in each category below.

Title of Fiction Book: _______________________________

Yummy Words

Sleepy Words

Happy Words

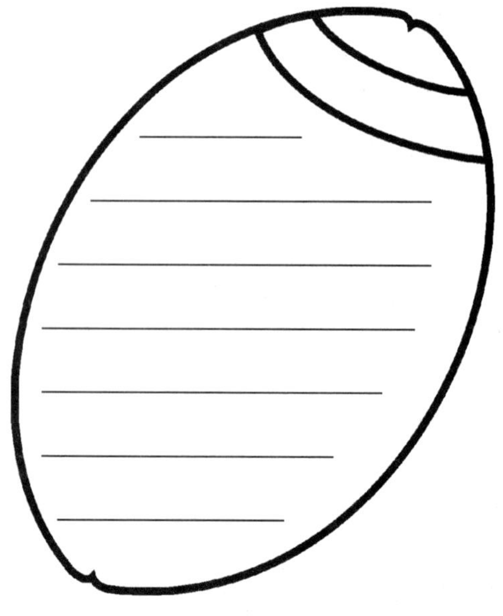

Active Words

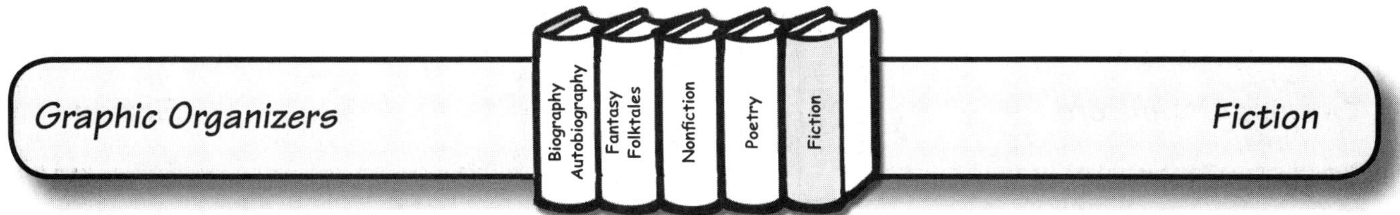

Fishy Book Report

Directions: Use the book-report form to tell more about your favorite fiction book.

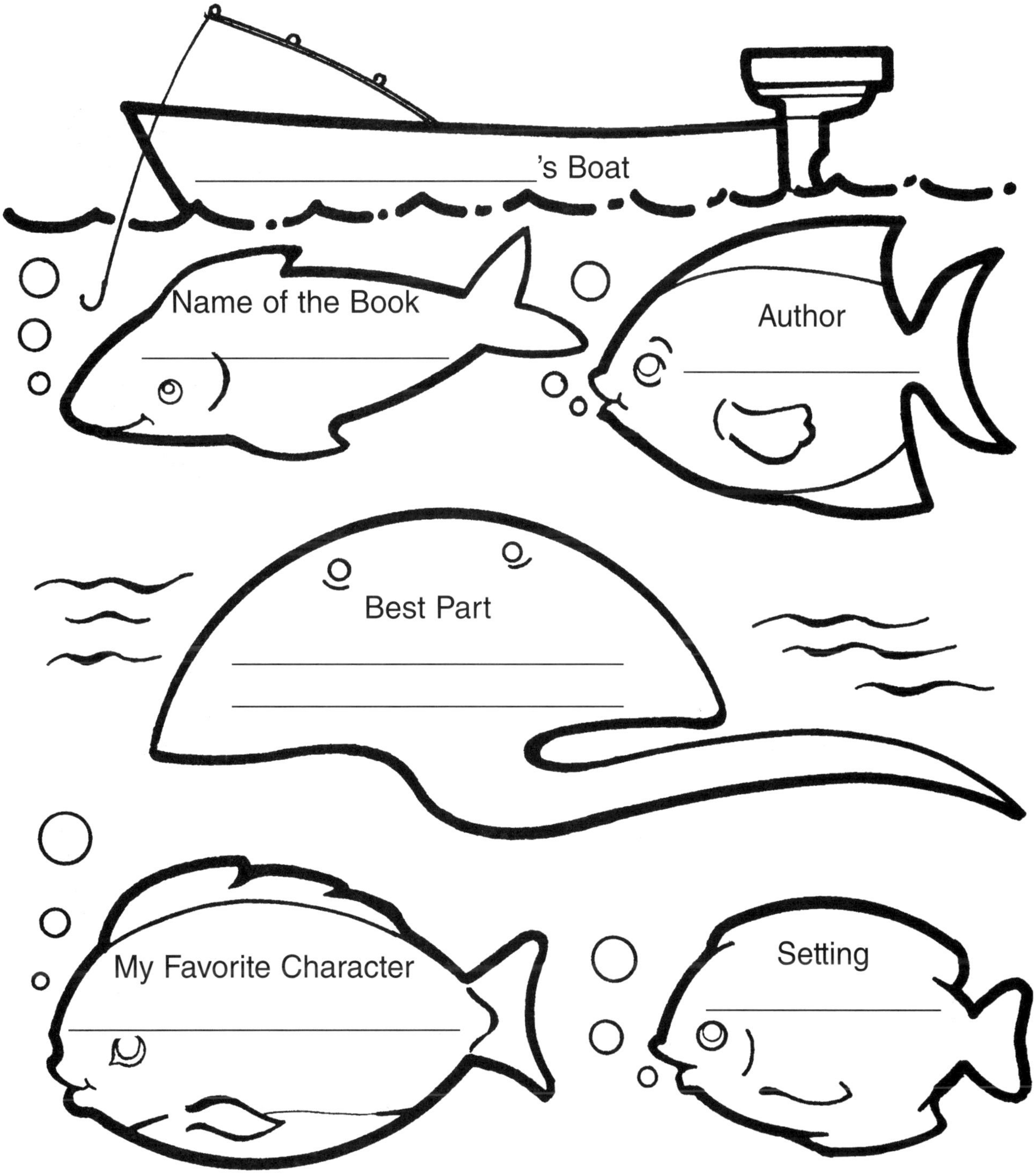

Book Report Pyramid I

Directions: Use the pyramid below to organize a book report for your fiction book.

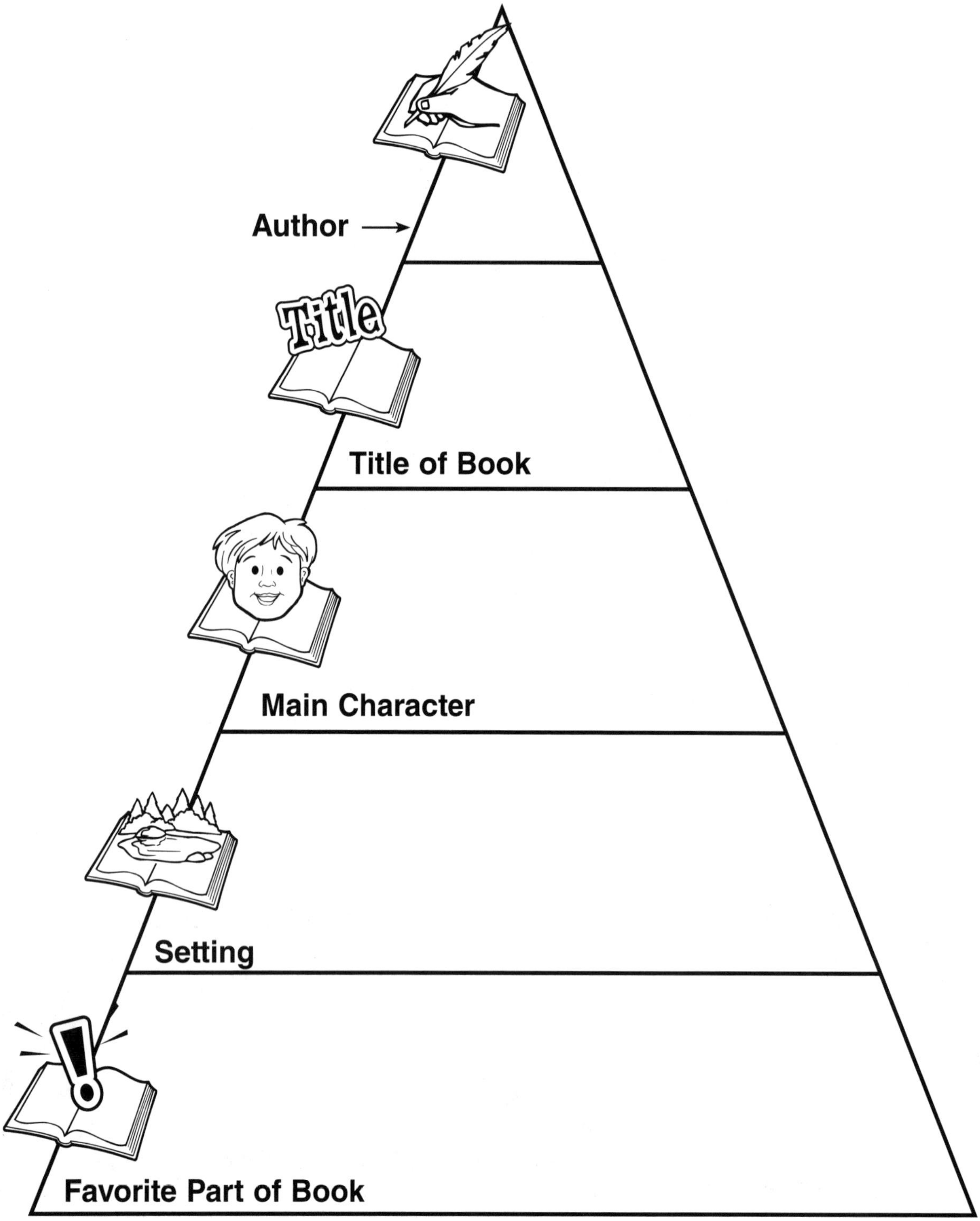

Author →

Title of Book

Main Character

Setting

Favorite Part of Book

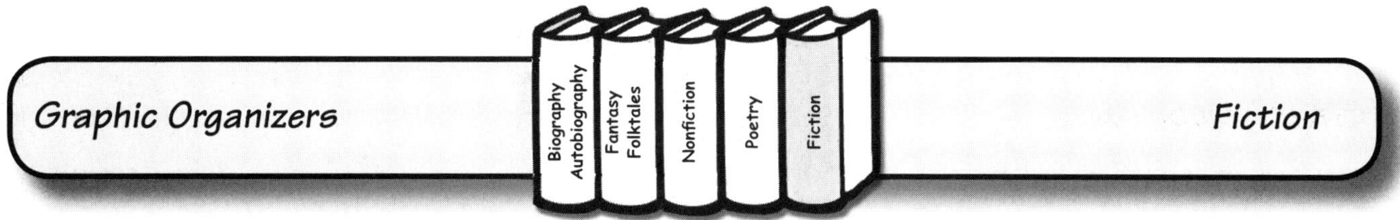

Book Report Pyramid II

Directions: Use the organizer to show how much you know about your fiction book.

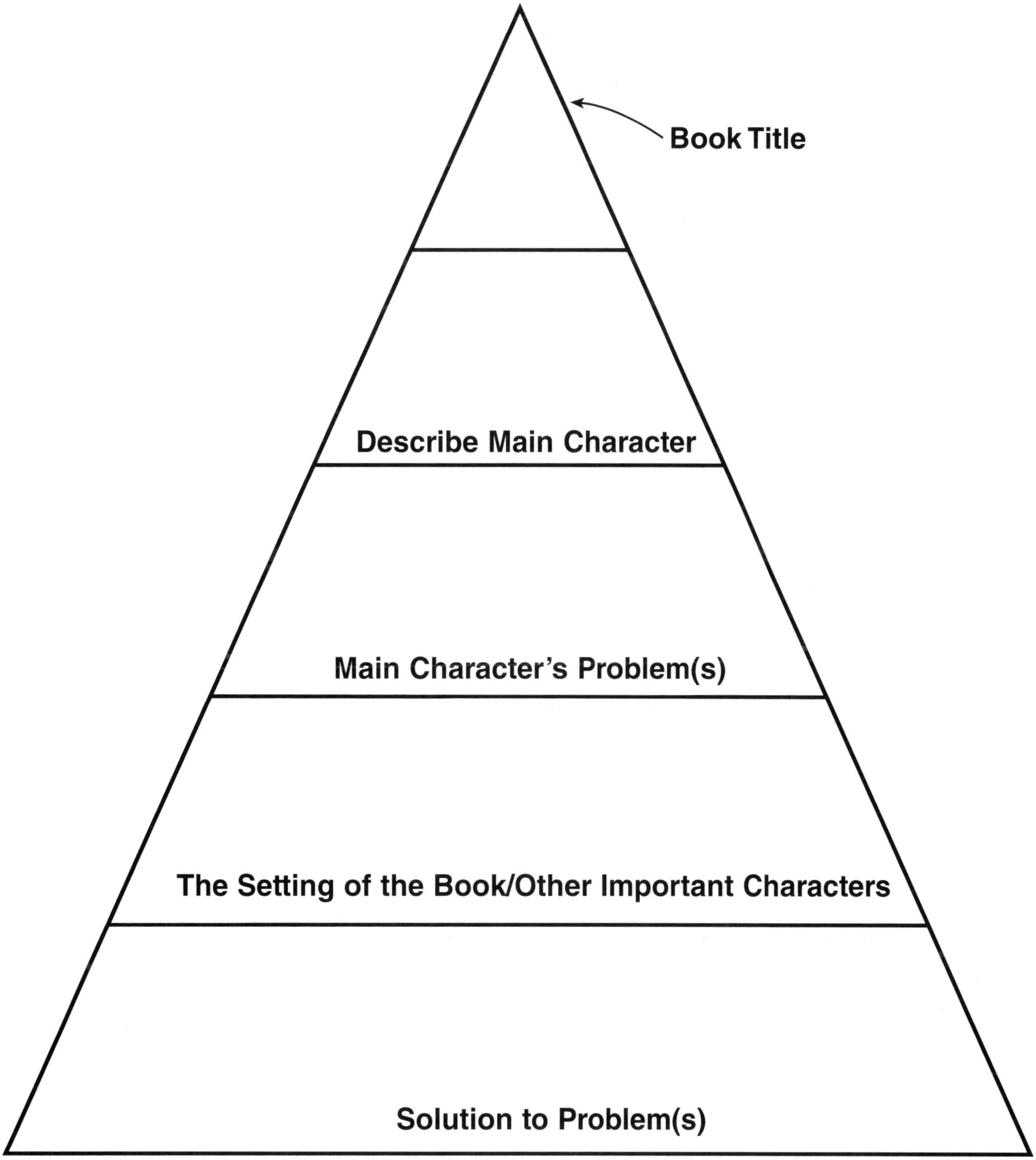

Book Title

Describe Main Character

Main Character's Problem(s)

The Setting of the Book/Other Important Characters

Solution to Problem(s)

Story Pyramid

Directions: Use the story pyramid to help you organize information from a short story.

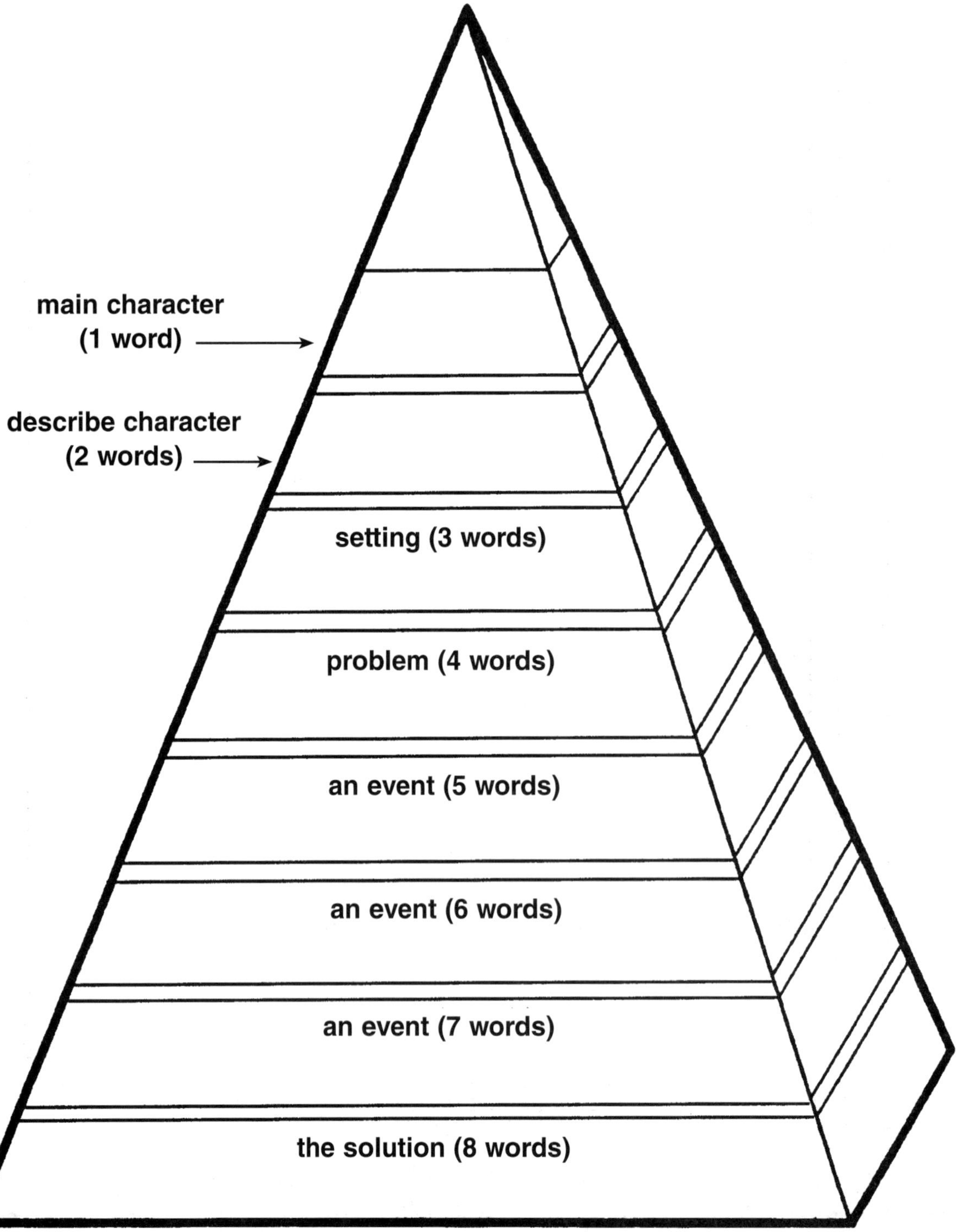

main character (1 word)

describe character (2 words)

setting (3 words)

problem (4 words)

an event (5 words)

an event (6 words)

an event (7 words)

the solution (8 words)

Book Cover

Directions: Design a new book cover for a favorite fiction book. Be sure to include the title and author of the book you have chosen.

Four "W" Questions

Directions: Tell about your fiction book by filling in the outlines below.

Who are the characters?

What is the title?

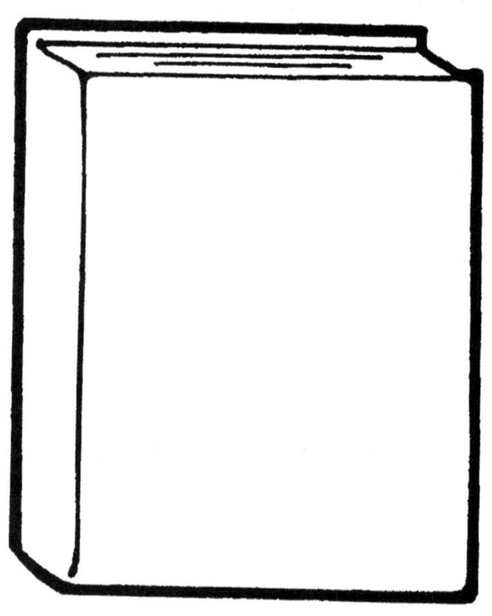

When did the story take place?

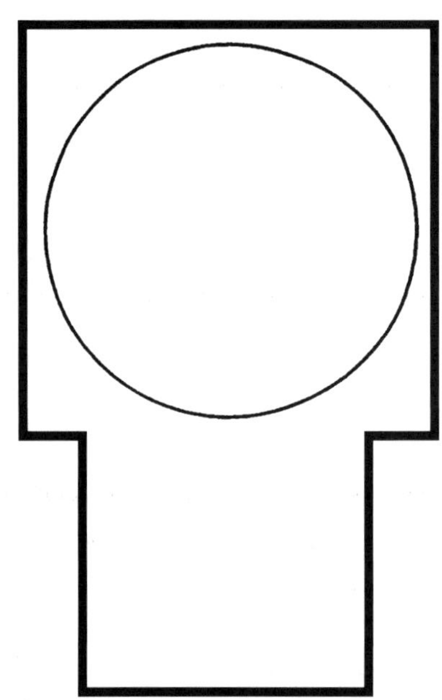

Where is the setting?

Putting Your Book in Order

Directions: Think about what happened in a fiction book you have read. Write those events in the order they occurred in the book. Be sure to summarize, or give a short description of, the events.

Book Title: ____

More with Sequencing

Directions: Practice putting the events from a fiction book in order by using the flow chart below. Begin by writing the title of the book on the top line. Then write or draw the events inside the circles in the order they happened.

Title: ____

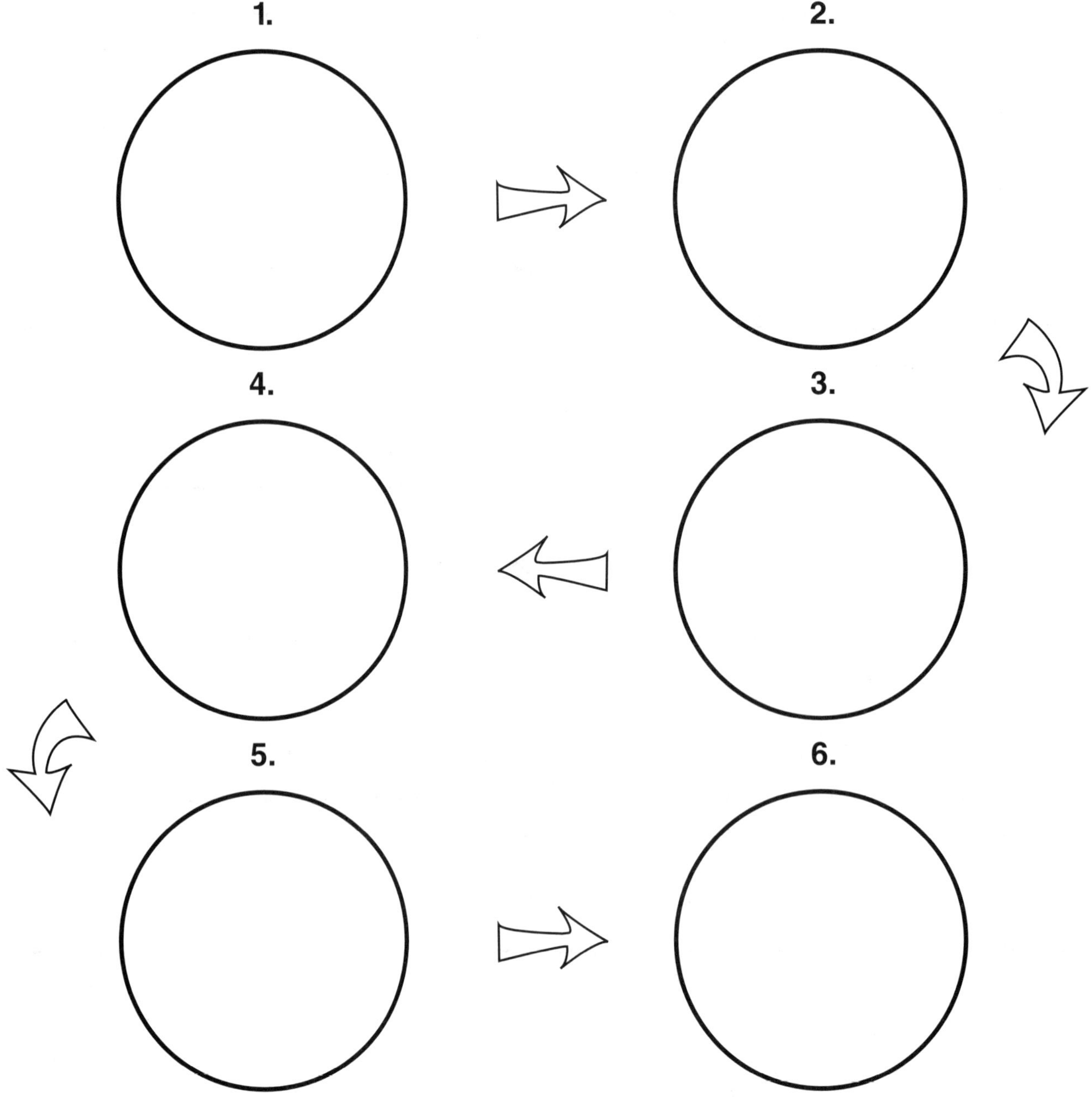

Flow Chart

Directions: Choose a fiction book you have recently read. Then outline the order of events on the chart. Be sure to place the events in the order they happened in the story.

Book Title: _______________________________

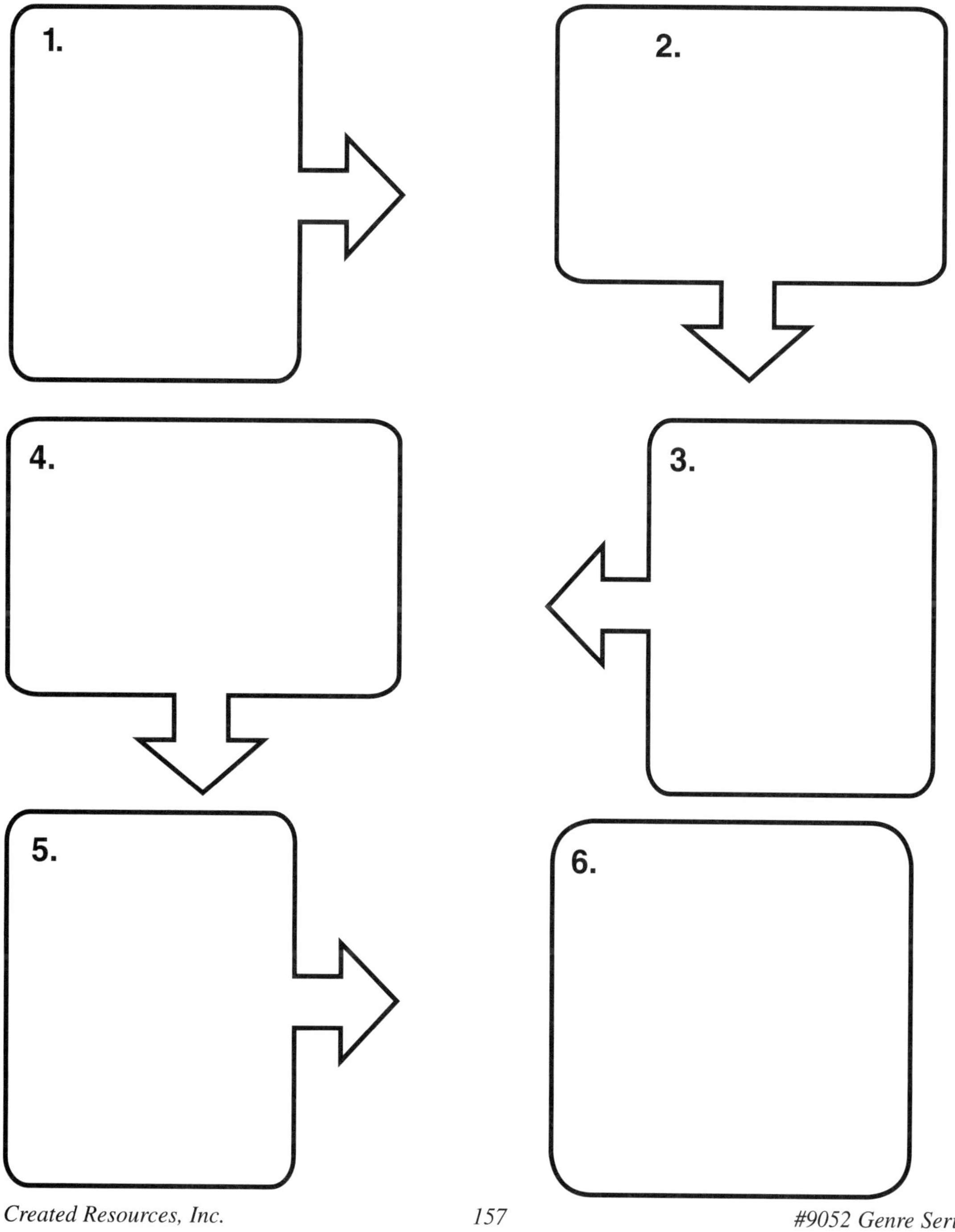

1.

2.

4.

3.

5.

6.

Teaching Cause and Effect

Use the organizer below to help you learn about cause and effect.

Directions: Use a story you have just finished reading with your class to complete the cause-and-effect chart. First, think of an important event in the story you read. Write the *cause* of the event in the first box. Write an *effect*, or result, of the event in the second box. Write the *final effect* of the action or event in the third box.

Book Title: ____

Cause
(action or event)

Effect
(result of the action)

Final Effect
(result of the action)

More Cause and Effect

Directions: Think of the events in a fiction book you have recently read. Then complete the cause-and-effect chart below.

Title: ____

Which caused

Which caused

Which caused

Which caused

Compare and Contrast

When you *compare* things, you are showing how two things are the same or alike. When you *contrast* things, you are showing how two things are different or not alike.

Directions: Choose two fiction characters you know very well. Write the name of one character underneath the left circle. Write the name of the second character underneath the right circle.

In the left circle, write five things that are unique to that character. In the right circle, write five things that are unique to that character. Where the two circles connect, write five things the characters have in common.

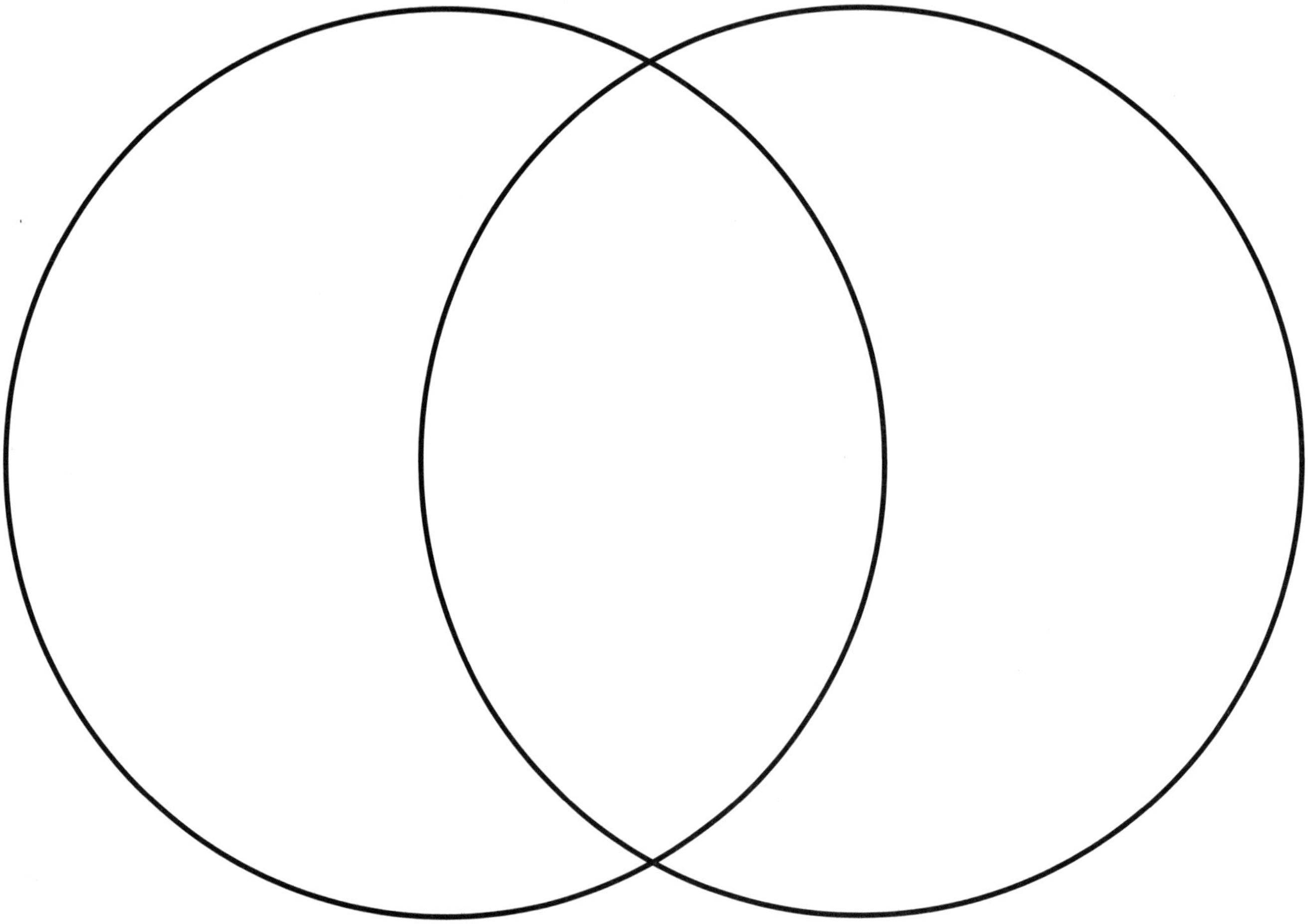

Character's Name   **Character's Name**

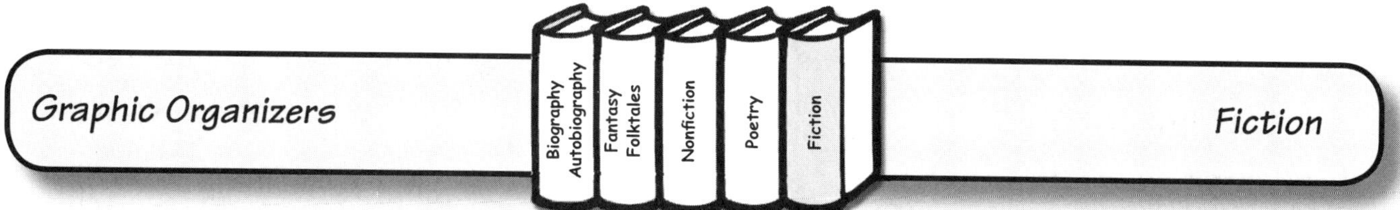

Critical Thinking and Characters

In fiction books, characters are often faced with problems that must be solved before they can move on in the story. Use a fiction book you have just begun to read to complete the organizer below.

Directions: As you begin to read a new book, think about the main character. What problems is the character facing? Complete the chart below as you read the book.

Book Title: _______________________________

The character's problem is . . . ➤

I think the problem will be solved . . . ➤

The problem was solved . . . ➤

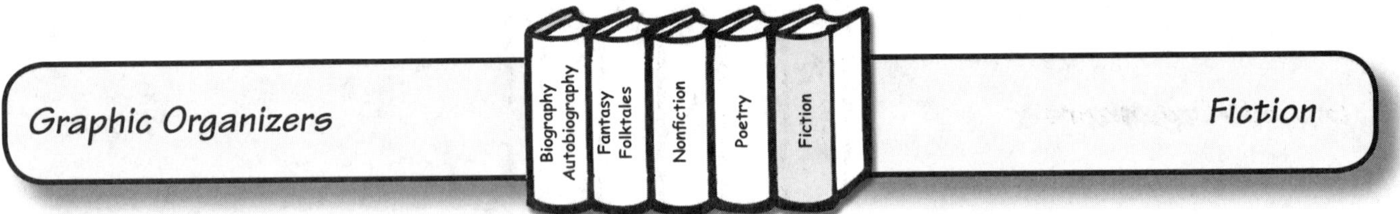

What a Character!

Directions: Use the organizer to tell more about a favorite fiction character.

Is this the main character or another character?

What do you like/dislike about this character?

What are the character's physical features? (What does he, she, or it look like?)

Character's Name

____

How does this character behave?

What are the character's weaknesses?

What are the character's strengths?

Fun with Characters

Directions: Choose a fiction book you really like. Think about two of the main characters in the book. Use the two main characters in a comic strip that you create. Draw the characters in a scene from the book. As you draw out your scene, be sure to include the words that would be said by your characters.

Book Title: ____

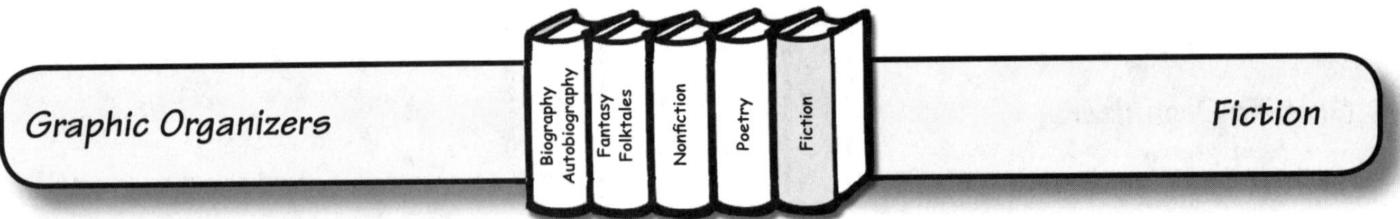

Character Connection

Sample Organizer

Directions: Use the organizer on page 165 to help you see the relationship between the characters in your story.

Begin by writing the name of the main character on the drawing of the person in the center. Then think of other characters your main character knew in the story. Write their names in the circles on the page and show how those other characters are connected to the main character.

Example:

Title: Jack and the Beanstalk

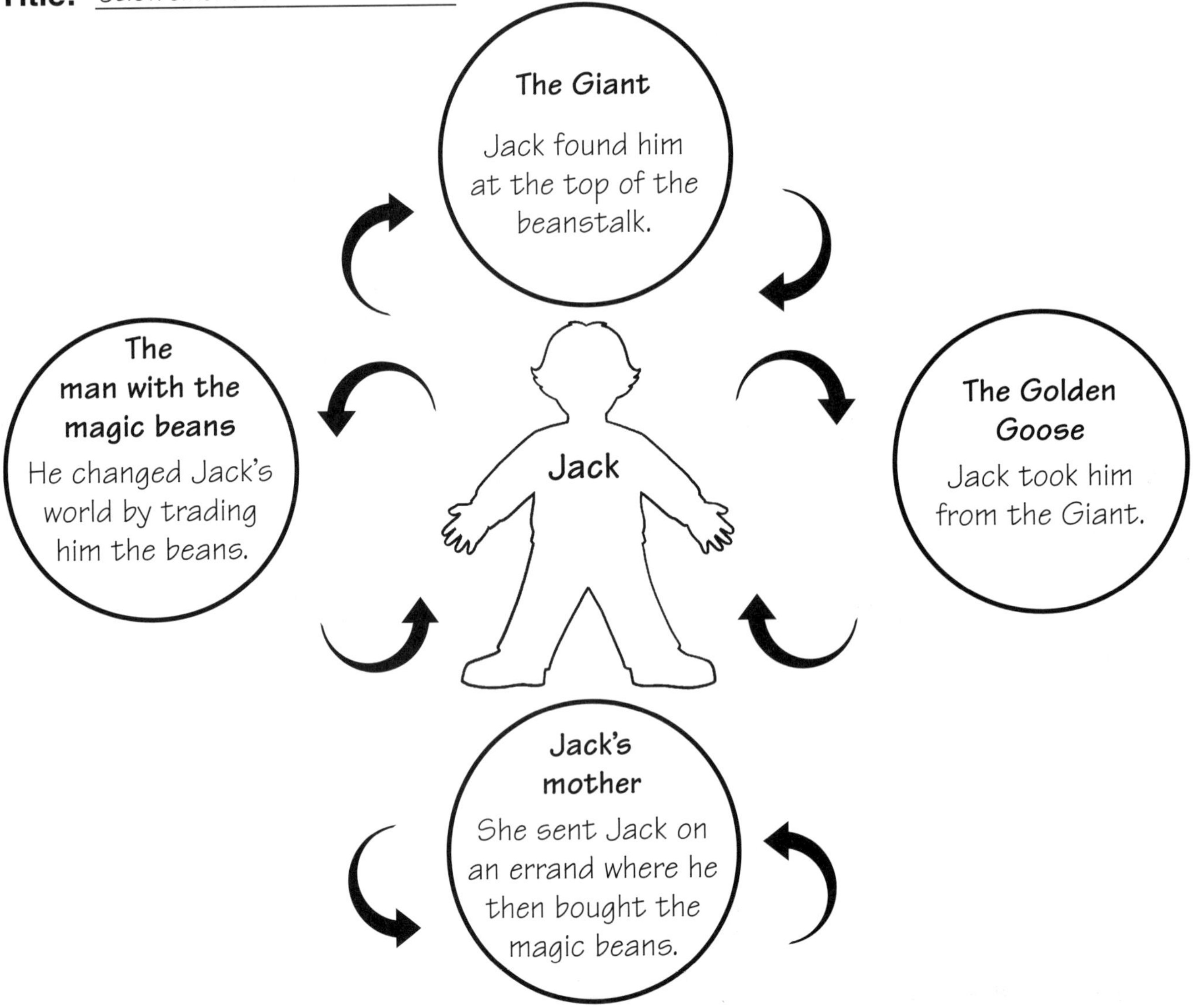

The Giant

Jack found him at the top of the beanstalk.

The man with the magic beans

He changed Jack's world by trading him the beans.

The Golden Goose

Jack took him from the Giant.

Jack

Jack's mother

She sent Jack on an errand where he then bought the magic beans.

Character Connection

Title: ____

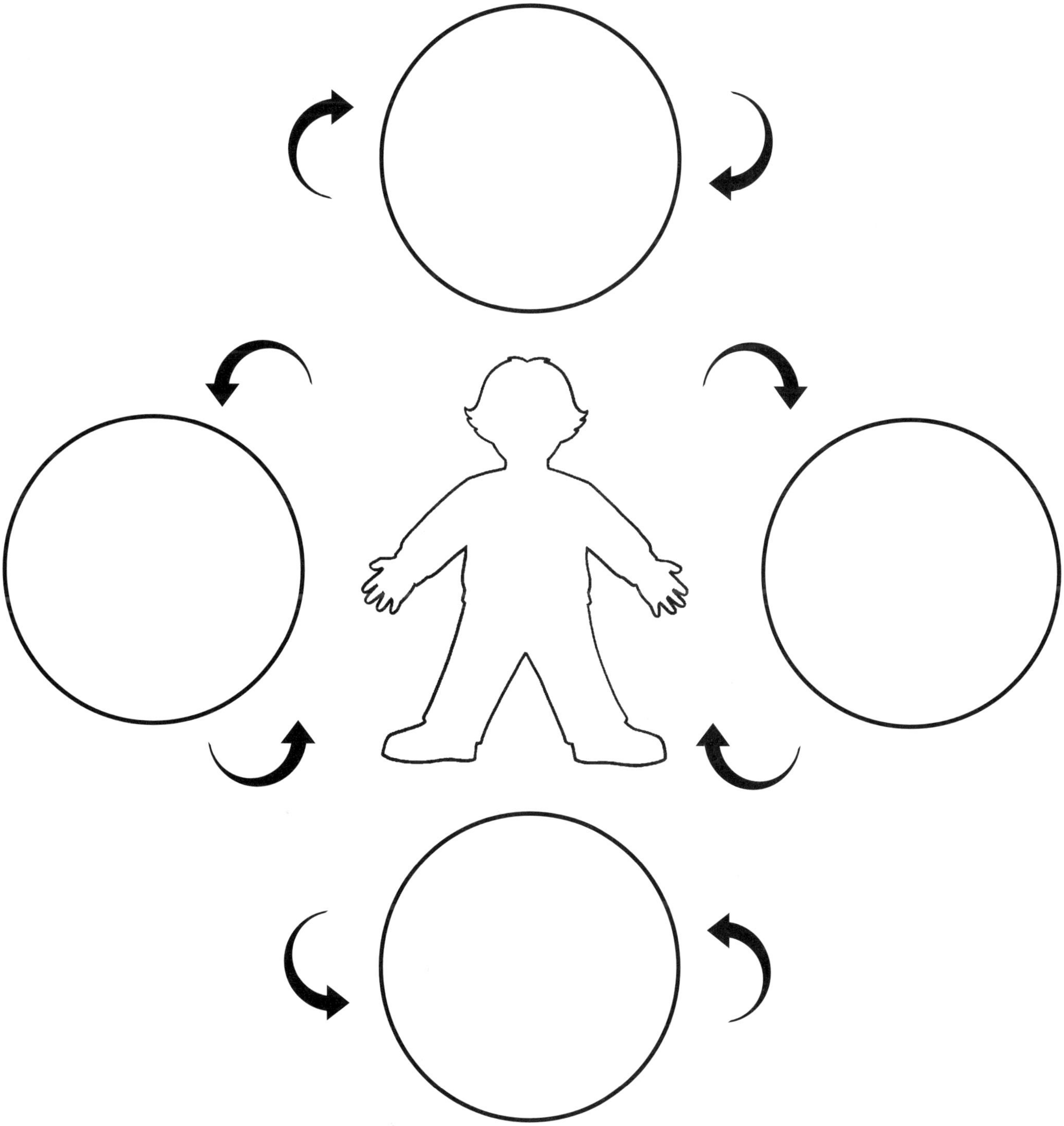

Drawing the Setting

Directions: Write the name of a fiction book you have recently read. Draw the main setting in the center rectangle. Draw the other settings found in the book in the remaining squares. If you need more squares, use the back of the paper.

Book Title: ____

Alike and Different

Directions: Choose two fiction books you have recently read. Write the titles of the books on the lines provided.

- ✎ Write the ways the two books are alike in the "Alike" column.
- ✎ Write the ways the two books are different in the "Different" column.

Book Title #1: ____

Book Title #2: ____

Alike	Different

Answer Key

Page 6

1. b
2. a
3. b
4. a
5. b

Page 7

Nonfiction: 1, 2, 5, 6, 10

Fiction: 3, 4, 7, 8, 9

Page 11

1. N
2. N
3. F
4. F
5. F
6. F
7. N
8. F

Page 12

1. fiction
2. not fiction
3. not fiction
4. fiction
5. fiction
6. not fiction
7. fiction
8. not fiction

Page 13

Green haystacks: 1, 2, 4, 6, 9

Yellow haystacks: 3, 5, 7, 8

Page 14

1. False
2. True
3. True
4. False
5. False
6. True
7. False
8. False

Page 20

1. c
2. e
3. a
4. b
5. d

Page 21

Part I

1. creation
2. evolution
3. revolution
4. solution

Part II

Answers will vary.

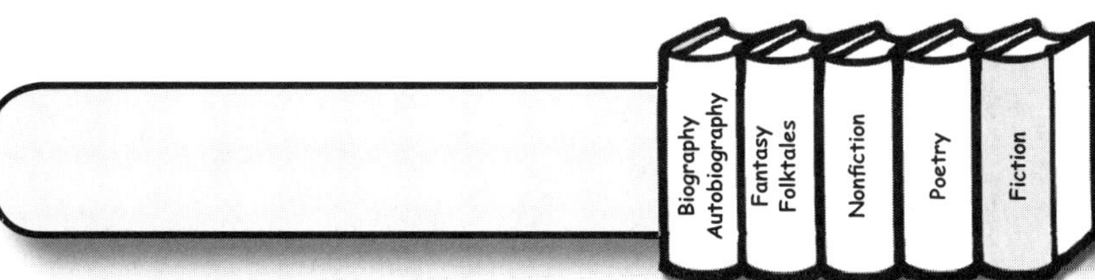

Answer Key *(cont.)*

Page 22

Found in fiction: 1, 5, 6, 7

Found in nonfiction: 2, 3, 4, 8

Page 25

1. Irene is nervous about dancing in front of so many people at her dance recital.

2. Irene wanted to tell her mother about her dream.

3. It made her feel like she could dance without any mistakes.

4. Irene's costume arrived.

5. Irene smiled because there were red shoes with her costume.

Page 26

1. b

2. b

3. a

4. b

5. b

Page 27

1. b

2. a

3. b

4. a

Page 28

1. Mike was different from other cats because he had a stubby tail.

2. Mike's feelings changed because he realized having a stubby tail could be a good thing.

3. The main point of the story is to be happy with who you are. This story could teach you to not be unhappy with something about yourself that you can't change.

Page 31

1. Some children are trying to give a muddy dog a bath.

2. A child is trying to roller blade, but he is falling down a lot.

3. A mouse is hungry, and he is staring at the food.

4. A child is trying to make a sandwich, but he's also making a big mess.

Page 32

1. Yes. This could be for a fiction story because there are many imaginary things in the picture.

2. Answers will vary.

3. Answers will vary.

4. a

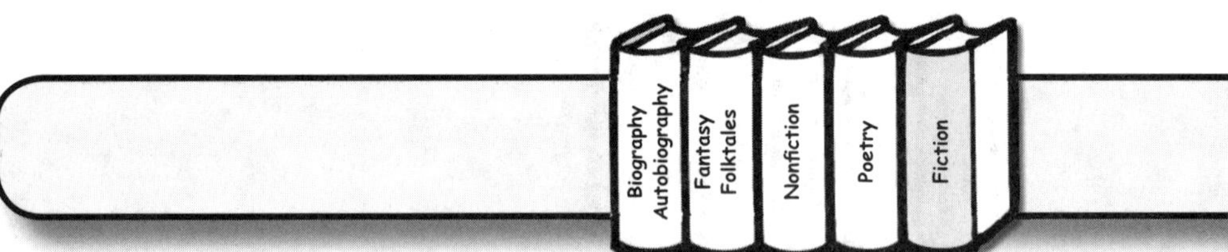

Answer Key *(cont.)*

Page 33

1. c

2. a

3. d

Page 34

1. a

2. a

3. b

4. a

Page 35

1. She tried to understand and not be upset.

2. Answers will vary.

3. She squeals with delight.

Page 44

1. Orville and Wilbur Wright (the Wright brothers)

2. They invented the airplane.

3. It includes a real, historical event with real people, but it also includes a fictional character.

Page 46

1. a   4. a

2. b   5. a

3. b   6. a

Page 47

1. fantasy

2. not fantasy

3. fantasy

4. fantasy

Page 48

1. The girl wanted her sister's smaller feet.

2. The next day she had smaller feet.

3. She did not like them.

Page 49

1. mystery/suspense

2. not a mystery/suspense

3. mystery/suspense

4. mystery/suspense

Page 50

1. True

2. True

3. False

4. False

5. False

Page 51

1. b   4. a

2. a   5. a

3. b   6. a

Answer Key *(cont.)*

Page 54

1. Answers will vary.

2. the rat

3. The rat turns into a prince, and they get married.

Page 57

1. It is in Emily's bedroom in the present time.

2. Answers will vary

3. It goes back to the past. Answers will vary.

4. Answers will vary.

Page 63

1. Yes. Answers will vary.

2. Answers will vary.

3. Answers will vary.

4. Answers will vary.

5. Answers will vary.

Page 69

1. The class had to leave the building.

2. A teacher burnt a piece of toast.

3. They were worried that their class would burn down. They were worried about their pet hamster, Jason.

4. The fire department and members of the police department showed up at the school.

5. They were surprised but relieved.

6. Answers will vary.

Page 77

1. Nate, Tim, Kerry

2. Kerry, Tim, Nate

3. 3, 1, 2

4. Kerry

5. Tim

6. Nate

Page 78

1. Sunday, Monday, Tuesday, Wednesday, Thursday, Friday, Saturday

2. January, February, March, April, May, June, July, August, September, October, November, December

3. Answers will vary.

4. Earth, Jupiter, Mars, Mercury, Neptune, Saturn, Uranus, Venus

Page 81

Correctly capitalized: 2, 3, 4, 7, 8

Page 82

1. C

2. Once there was a shaggy, brown dog that liked playing in a large park.

3. The moon lit up the sky.

4. Princess Ayala lived in a rainbow castle.

5. C

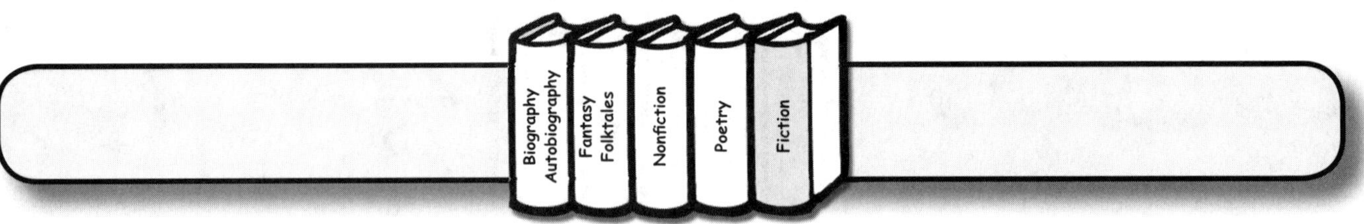

Answer Key *(cont.)*

Page 83

Fish that are correct: 2, 3, 4, 6, 7, 8

Page 84

1. Once upon a time there lived two princesses.

2. The two princesses were very good friends.

3. Have you ever had a very best friend?

4. How wonderful it is to have a good friend!

5. The two princesses grew up and married two brothers.

6. What do you think was special about the two brothers?

7. Each of the two brothers was a prince.

8. How amazing that each girl would fall in love with a prince!

Page 85

Ten mistakes:

They thought he was friendly.

He liked to listen to everyone's secrets.

He could easily hear the lions talking.

But do you know what else he did?

How terrible!

Telling the monkeys was a bad idea because the monkeys were a bit tricky.

They wanted to teach the bird a lesson.

So do you know what the monkeys decided to do?

Soon, Mr. Parrot flew near.

The next day, no one would talk to him.

Page 89

Subjects:

1. Kristen

2. cake

3. Kristen

4. Allison

5. parents

6. Kristen

7. Balloons

8. Allison

Page 93

1. Once

2. dog

3. park

4. animals

5. pretty

6. butterfly

7. was

8. Today

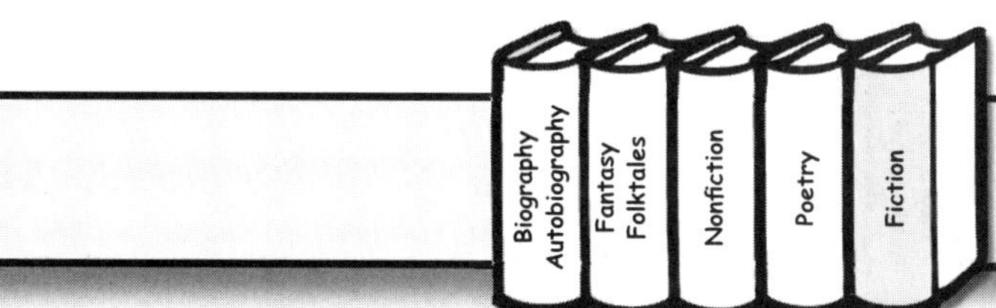

Answer Key *(cont.)*

Page 94

1. fir — The dog got fur all over the couch.

2. flour — A daisy is my favorite flower.

3. petal — If you want to go faster, just pedal harder.

4. plain — I flew home on a plane.

5. ate — We had eight guests for supper.

6. four — We did all of this for you.

Page 95

1. blue

2. right

3. high

4. be

5. steak

6. sail

7. tick

8. cent or scent

9. days

10. die

Challenge: kernel

Page 96

1. Goldilocks went to the house, opened the door, and sat down at the table.

2. There were three bowls of porridge, three spoons, and three glasses.

3. She tried the porridge from one bowl, tried the porridge from the second bowl, and tried the porridge from the third bowl.

4. The porridge in the three bowls was too hot, too cold, and just right.

5. After the meal Goldilocks was full, tired, and sleepy.

6. She left the kitchen, climbed the stairs, and went into the bedroom.

7. She tried the first bed, the second bed, and the third bed.

8. The mattresses on the bed were hard, soft, and just right.

9. Goldilocks lay down, closed her eyes, and went to sleep.

10. Suddenly, the door opened and Father Bear, Mother Bear, and Baby Bear entered the room.

11. Imagine their surprise to see that someone had eaten their porridge, someone had been in their house, and someone was still there!

12. Goldilocks woke up, screamed, and ran out of the house.

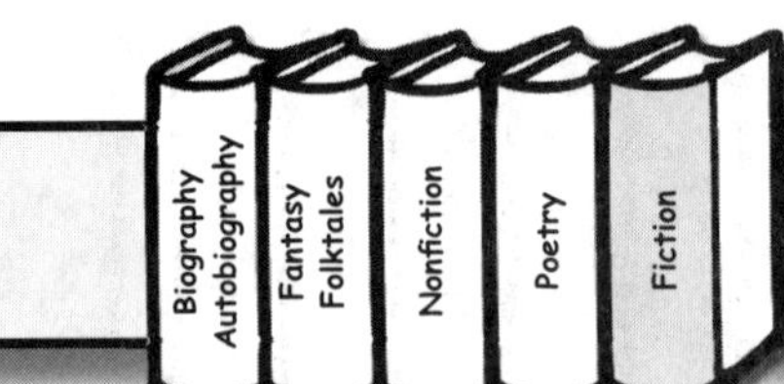

Answer Key *(cont.)*

Page 99

Eight mistakes:

1. African (capitalization)
2. sky (spelling)

Page 99 *(cont.)*

3. beautiful (spelling)
4. sad. (ending punctuation)
5. I (capitalization)
6. light (spelling)
7. night. (ending punctuation)
8. more. (ending punctuation)

Page 101

1. b
2. a
3. c
4. a
5. c

Page 102

1. True
2. False
3. False
4. True
5. False
6. False
7. False

8. True
9. True
10. False

Page 105

1. Homestead
2. He sounded like a snake. He made an exaggerated "s" sound.
3. snakes
4. He was missing.
5. because he was an adult
6. Sam's boots and belt buckle
7. because Sam always wore them
8. He went to the big city.
9. because he was lonely
10. No. He had friends like Tommy and Tommy's mother.

Page 106

1. Answers will vary.
2. Sam and Tommy
3. Answers will vary.
4. Everyone needs a friend.

Page 109

Fiction:

The man in the moon winked at me.

The horse and chariot helped the sun move across the sky.

Answer Key *(cont.)*

Page 109 *(cont.)*

My sister's fairy godmother turned her into a princess.

The characters came out of the video game and played with my toys.

My stomach yelled, "I'm hungry!"

The farmer fed his three unicorns.

Nonfiction:

The moon comes out at night.

The sun warmed up the Earth.

My sister is a pest.

The video game was fun.

My stomach growled because I was hungry

The farmer fed his three horses.

Page 110

Colored gophers: 1, 2, 5, 6, 7, 8

Page 111

1. b
2. b
3. b
4. a
5. a
6. b

Page 113

1. Carlos liked to pick up shells.

2. Carlos first saw the creature on the beach.

3. Mary liked to watch the birds.

4. Carlos found a shark.

5.–8. Answers will vary.

Page 114

1. The above story is nonfiction.

2. Because the information is all true; it is filled with facts.

3. Yes, an author could write both a fiction and a nonfiction story about snakes.

Page 117

1. pretend
2. imagination
3. historical
4. fiction
5. Nonfiction
6. library

Page 119

Light bulbs that should be colored:

A fiction author can use his imagination.

Fiction is the opposite of nonfiction.

Fairy tales are a type of fiction.

There are many types of fiction stories.

A dictionary is not a fiction book.

Fantasy books are a type of fiction.

Answer Key *(cont.)*

Page 121

1. a
2. b
3. b
4. a
5. b
6. a
7. a
8. a

Bibliography

Kissel, Jessica M. Dubin. *Ready to Go Lessons: Reading and Writing.* Teacher Created Resources, Inc., 2006.

Petersen, Casey Null. *Graphic Organizers, Grades K–3.* Teacher Created Resources, Inc., 2004.

Russell, Shelle. *Daily Warm-Ups: Reading, Grade 2.* Teacher Created Resources, Inc., 2006.

Teacher Created Resources Staff. *Reading Comprehension, Grade 3.* Teacher Created Resources, Inc. 2002. Reprinted, 2007.

Teacher Created Resources Staff. *Reading Comprehension, Grade 2.* Teacher Created Resources, Inc. 2002. Reprinted, 2007.